DATE DUE

First published in September 2006

A catalogue record for this book is available from the British Library

ISBN 1 84425 311 2

Library of Congress catalog card no. 2006924133

Published by Haynes Publishing,
Sparkford, Yeovil, Somerset BA22 7JJ, UK

Tel: 01963 442030 Fax: 01963 440001
Int. tel: +44 1963 442030 Int. fax: +44 1963 440001
E-mail: sales@haynes.co.uk
Website: www.haynes.co.uk

Haynes North America, Inc.,
861 Lawrence Drive, Newbury Park,
California 91320, USA

Designed by Richard Parsons

Printed and bound in England
by J. H. Haynes & Co. Ltd, Sparkford

WARNING
While every effort is taken to ensure the accuracy of the information given in this book, no liability can be accepted by the author or publishers for any loss, damage or injury caused by errors in, or omissions from the information given.

Photograph Credits

AA P38 top **Alfa Romeo** P9 bottom **Avon Tyres** P111 top **BMW** P82, P85 top and bottom right, P101, P104 **Bosch** P85 upper left, P92, P93 bottom, P114, P115 top **BP** P73 top **Brembo** P107 top **Comma** P118, P124, P126 **Continental Tyres** P110, P113 **Ford** P10 top, P44, P66 bottom, P84, P85 lower left, P105 bottom, P106 **Green Flag** P69 **Haynes** P20 top, P28, P30, P31, P32, P33, P34, P35, P40, P45, P47 bottom, P49 top, P53 bottom, P54-55, P57 bottom, P71 bottom, P75, P79, P81, P86, P87, P88, P89 lower, P90, P92 upper, P95 top, P96, P97, P98, P99, P102, P103, P105 upper, P107 lower pair, P108, P109, P111 bottom, P115 bottom, P121 bottom, P123, P127, P128, P129, P130-139, P148-156 **Hella** P154 **Honda** P120, P144 **IAM** P67 **iStockphoto** P13, P14, P18, P21 top, P25, P36 OR P37 (possibly - check), P38 bottom, P39, P47 top, P51 top, P56, P58, P59, P60, P61, P63, P66 top, P72, P73 bottom, P74, P78, P80, P89 top, P121 top, P125, P145, P147, P157, P162, P166 **Iveco** P41 top **John Wickersham** P53 top **Manheim Auctions** P19, P21, P24 **Maybach** P117 bottom **Mazda** P10, P16, P26, P140, P142 **Megular's** P122 **Mercedes-Benz** P85 middle right, P100 bottom **Merlin Consumer Publishing Ltd** P20 bottom **Mille Miglia** P117 middle **Mitsubishi** P52 **Motorsport Vision** P68 **NGK** P95 bottom **Nissan** P6, P8 **Ontime Rescue and Recovery** P71 top **Peugeot** P9 top, P91 bottom **RAC** P36 OR P37 (possibly - check), P41 middle and bottom **Renault** P10 bottom, P29, P62, P77 **Skoda** P51 bottom **SMART** P117 top **Suzuki** P11 top **Toyota** P11 bottom **Thule** P48 **Vauxhall** P9 middle, P10 middle, P22, P42, P49 bottom, P50, P70, P91 top, P112 bottom, P116, P143, P159, P164, P167 **Volkswagen** P112 top, P160 **Volvo** P65 **What Car?** P12, P46, P64

the Car book

Haynes

Everything you need to know about owning, enjoying and maintaining your car

Steve Rendle

Buying
and selling

Using
your car

Getting
on the road

Know
your car

Caring for
your car

Appendix

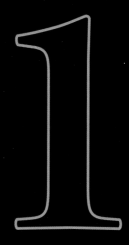

Buying
and selling

Which car?

When you set out to buy a car, there's now an almost bewildering variety of types and models to choose from, but by doing a little research, and setting yourself a budget, you'll be able to narrow the choice down to a few models, or maybe even a single model that fits your needs.

Diesel or petrol?

Before you start to think about which model of car is going to suit your needs best, you need first to choose between petrol and diesel engines. Diesel engines are generally more economical than petrol engines, and modern diesel engines are every bit as powerful as their petrol counterparts, if not more powerful in some cases. Diesel engines are also considered to be less harmful to the environment because they produce less harmful exhaust emissions. Overall fuel costs will be lower for a diesel-engined car, but the initial purchase price is likely to be higher, although this isn't always the case. In the end the choice of engine type comes down to personal preference.

'First' cars

If you've just learnt to drive, or you're just starting to learn and you're looking for your first car, the choice can be baffling. For most people choosing a first car, the most important considerations are the cost of the car itself and the cost of the insurance, as insurance can be very expensive for newly qualified drivers. Often, an insurance policy for a young or inexperienced driver can cost as much as the car itself – sometimes even more!

Generally, the smaller the car's engine, the cheaper the car will be to insure, so probably the best bet for a first car is a small hatchback or saloon with a reasonably small engine. This doesn't mean that you have to have a boring car, but it really does pay to get a few quotes for insurance on the type of car you're thinking of buying before you take the plunge. Unless you have very deep pockets, it's probably best not to rush out and buy an exotic powerful sports car!

ABOVE Peugeot's stylish 206 has proved very popular and is an ideal first car

BELOW The Vauxhall Astra – a good example of a typical modern Hatchback

Hatchbacks and saloons

These are probably the most practical all-rounder cars for everyday use, and there's a huge range of cars to choose from in this class, of all sizes, shapes, specifications and prices.

Hatchbacks offer the practicality of a one-piece 'tailgate' for easy loading and the transport of large or awkward loads, whereas saloons generally have a lower rear-end profile at the expense of load-carrying space. Both are suitable for longer-distance driving and spacious enough to allow four adults to travel in comfort, with a reasonable amount of luggage. There are more hatchback models available than saloons – some manufacturers don't produce saloon versions of their mainstream models.

Hatchbacks and saloons are generally amongst the cheapest cars to insure. They're also generally the cheapest to buy, as they are plentiful and there are more models to choose from than any other class of car on the market. Engine capacities vary widely, but most models are designed with overall cost of ownership in mind.

BELOW The Alfa Romeo 159 is arguably one of the most stylish saloon designs available

Estate cars

Estate cars are ideal if load carrying is an important consideration. There are fewer estate car models to choose from, but on the used market you'll often find that they cost little more than their hatchback equivalents because there's generally less demand for estate models. The current trend for MPVs has reduced the demand for estate cars, so the choice of estate models available has also narrowed. Estate cars are ideal if you carry a lot of luggage, or perhaps a dog, on a regular basis.

Although it may be stating the obvious, bear in mind that some estate models are significantly longer than their hatchback equivalents, which means that they may take up more space when parking – worth thinking about if you intend to park the car on your drive or in a garage.

Sports cars

These are most fun cars to own, but the least practical and the most expensive to insure – the ultimate 'heart over head purchase'! Sports cars are relatively expensive to run, as the maintenance costs tend to be higher than mainstream models, as does the fuel consumption. As well as speed, most sports cars offer higher than average levels of grip, and are designed to make driving fun.

Although there's a reasonable range of models to choose from, you'll pay more for a sports car than for other types because there are fewer available and they're more desirable.

You'll normally find better deals on used sports cars in the autumn or winter, when they're harder to sell because demand is lower.

ABOVE Ford's Mondeo Estate is one of the most popular estate cars on the market

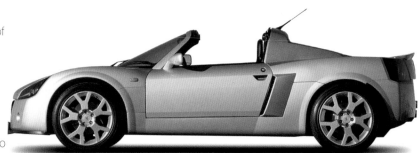

People carriers (MPVs)

People carriers, also known as Multi-Purpose Vehicles (MPVs), are now one of the most popular types of car on the road. They're ideally suited to large families, and families with children. MPVs come in various shapes and sizes, from high-roofed variants of hatchback models to full-blown van-based people carriers able to seat seven occupants in comfort, and there are models to suit most requirements and tastes.

As demand for MPVs is high, prices, both new and used, tend to be higher than for mainstream

hatchback and saloon models, and MPVs are also more expensive to insure.

If you're looking for the advantages of a slightly higher driving position, and therefore better visibility than a hatchback or saloon model, coupled with versatility for load and people carrying, then an MPV is a good option. One downside is that many MPVs have less than generous boot space – particularly if you have a full load of passengers. You may find that you need to use a roofbox with some models to increase the available luggage space.

ABOVE Vauxhall's stunning VX220 sports car will provide plenty of smiles per mile!

LEFT The Renault Espace is a good example of an MPV that can seat seven people in comfort

SUVs

Sports Utility Vehicles come in all shapes and sizes, and often have four-wheel drive. They're marketed as 'lifestyle' vehicles, aimed mainly at owners who need space to carry leisure equipment as well as passengers. Some SUVs have soft-tops to allow wind-in-the-hair motoring.

If you need space to carry cycles, fishing gear, etc, then an SUV may be the car for you. Some buyers opt for an SUV rather than a sports car.

As demand for SUVs is high, particularly during the summer months, prices, both new and used, tend to be higher than for mainstream hatchback and saloon models, and SUVs are also more expensive to insure.

4x4s

4x4s come in many shapes and sizes, and can be ideal for recreational use and for towing, although a pretty low percentage of 4x4s are ever used off-road. In fact some 4x4s are actually quite poor for off-road driving, and many are fitted with wheels and tyres aimed at road use.

If you're looking for a vehicle to tow a caravan or trailer regularly, or if you're likely to need to drive off-road occasionally, or regularly, then a 4x4 may fit your bill, although 4x4s are increasingly popular with families looking for a durable and stylish means of covering the school run.

4x4s are expensive to buy, expensive to run, and expensive to insure, so make sure that you do plenty of research into costs before taking the plunge. Also be aware that there are a lot of 'grey-import' 4x4s for sale, and although these can be affordable to buy, they won't be any cheaper to run, they're likely to be more expensive to insure than models 'officially' sold in the UK, and it can be difficult to obtain spare parts for some imported models.

ABOVE Suzuki's compact Jimny has proved a big hit as an affordable, fun SUV

BELOW Toyota's Landcruiser is equally at home off-road, towing, or on the school run

General buying advice

Before buying a car, do as much research as you can into the models that you're keen to look at. There are plenty of car magazines that will provide road-test information, often comparing similar models, and there are also a number of websites offering information and advice.

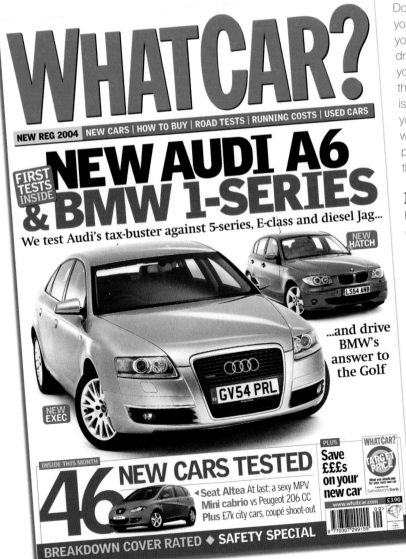

Don't be afraid to test-drive several cars to help you to decide on the model to go for, and if you're buying a used car it's a good idea to test-drive a few examples of the particular models you're interested in so that you can compare them and get an idea of whether a particular car is a good or poor example. Make sure that you're comparing like with like, for example a car with power steering will generally be easier to park than one without. Don't rush into buying the first car that you see.

Depreciation

For many people, the biggest cost involved in car ownership is depreciation. It's not until you decide to sell your car, or trade it in for a newer model, that you find out just how much money you've lost through depreciation since you bought it! The greatest depreciation usually takes place in the first year of a car's life, so bear this in mind if you're thinking of buying a new car. If you buy a year-old car from a reputable dealer it will have a similar guarantee to a brand-new model, but someone else will have paid for that first-year's depreciation.

Obviously, mileage has a big effect on depreciation, but there may not be much you can do to reduce the mileage you cover. Apart from mileage, the two main factors are the car's condition and service history, so to minimise depreciation look after your car, make sure that you have it serviced regularly, and keep the service record up to date.

Finance

Once you've decided how much you can afford to spend buying a car, you then have to decide how to finance your purchase. Depending on the car you have in mind, and your bank balance, you may be able to buy it outright from your savings without having to worry about finance, but if you do need to borrow money there are several options. The following advice will help you to decide which option best suits your situation and needs.

Whatever option you choose, always be sure to read the small print – there can be additional charges and conditions to a credit agreement that are not always obvious.

With loans and hire purchase agreements you will often be offered optional insurance to protect your payments if you become ill or unemployed. This insurance policy may provide you with peace of mind, but it can be expensive – you may do better to pay the insurance premium in one go at the start of the agreement, rather than adding it to your monthly payments.

Credit cards

If you're buying a car from a dealer, you will probably be able to pay for the car using a credit card, provided your credit limit will stand it. This is a relatively easy option, but make sure that the seller doesn't charge you a fee for paying by credit card, and if you're not intending to pay off the whole balance outstanding on your card in one go bear in mind that using a credit card could prove expensive, as you're likely to be paying a high interest rate. A personal loan may prove to be a better option.

LOW-COST LOANS

ABOVE Be wary when shopping around for a personal loan – some loans are not as 'low-cost' as they appear

Personal loans

A personal loan can be an affordable way to buy a car, as you'll effectively be able to spread the cost over a time period that suits you, and by shopping around you should be able to secure a loan at a competitive rate. Always try to deal with reputable banks or finance companies, and compare interest rates to make sure that you get a competitive deal. Be wary of small companies, or companies recommended by a dealer that you may not have heard of – some unscrupulous companies charge very high interest rates.

Once you know how much you can afford to borrow, and how much you can afford to pay, you just need to arrange for the loan to be paid into your bank account and you can then pay for the car.

Hire purchase

Hire purchase is also known as lease purchase, and is a method of paying for a car whereby you pay monthly payments to a finance company for an agreed period, and at the end of the agreed period the car becomes your property. During the hire purchase period – whilst you are making payments – the car belongs to the finance company, but you will normally be liable for any damage caused to the car during the agreed period.

Under a hire purchase agreement, you pay an initial deposit, followed by monthly payments (normally made up of a proportion of the money you owe plus interest) over an agreed period. At the end of the agreed period you will have the option of owning the car outright, although some lenders may charge a final fee, which can be high, so always check on the exact terms of the deal. With some types of hire purchase plan you will own

the car once all the outstanding instalments have been paid and there will be no extra fee to pay.

Always check the small print with hire purchase agreements – unfortunately there are unscrupulous companies operating who stipulate unreasonable conditions in their contracts, such as excessive charges if you break the terms of the agreement.

Contract hire

A contract hire agreement essentially enables you to have a new car, which you lease under a contract that will normally include all servicing and any unexpected repair bills. The car will always remain the property of the contract hire company.

Under a contract hire agreement, you'll make fixed monthly payments for the duration of the contract, and you won't have to pay any extra payments for servicing, repairs, or new components such as tyres. You'll obviously have to pay for fuel, and normally the cost of insurance will be your responsibility too – so always make sure that you have fully comprehensive cover, as you'll be liable if the car is damaged. At the end of the agreement, the car is returned to the contract hire company.

The advantage of a contract hire agreement is that you're making a fixed monthly payment for use of the car and all servicing, and you won't bear the cost of depreciation. The downsides of the agreement are that you won't own a car when the agreement comes to an end, and it can be a relatively expensive way for a private individual to run a car.

Many car manufacturers offer contract hire deals direct, so if this option appeals to you shop around for the best deal. The monthly payments can vary dramatically depending on the model of car concerned.

Warranties

Whenever you buy a new or second-hand car, a warranty should be included. Similarly, when you have any work carried out that work should be covered by a warranty.

The warranties provided with new cars are normally very comprehensive, and often include membership of one of the breakdown organisations. Three-year warranties are now commonplace, but you may be offered the chance to take out an 'extended warranty' on a new car. Always check carefully what's covered by an extended warranty and weigh this up against the cost – is there a claim limit, and is anything excluded? An extended warranty can be a very expensive way of buying peace of mind, especially if it ties you to having the car serviced by an authorised dealer.

When buying a second-hand car, always check what sort of warranty you're getting. Some warranties are very comprehensive, but you'll sometimes find that there's a maximum claim limit, which can be so low that it effectively limits claims to very minor problems. If you have to pay extra for a warranty, read the small print very carefully – you may find that the warranty isn't worth the extra cost, and if it's been included in the price of the car you may be able to negotiate a better deal if you say that you don't want the warranty.

Warranty and Service Guide

Buying new

Buying a new car is probably the most expensive option, but it is also the most secure – effectively you're protected against anything going wrong with the car. Most car manufacturers now provide a minimum of three years warranty with a new car, sometimes with unlimited mileage, and many manufacturers also provide a free membership of one of the breakdown organisations for the first year of ownership.

However, although a new car may seem like an attractive proposition, bear in mind that if you're a private buyer you'll lose money as soon as you buy it – the moment you drive the car away from the dealership it's worth less than you paid for it, unless you've managed to negotiate an exceptional deal. It's worthwhile considering buying a low-mileage demonstrator from a dealer as an alternative to a brand-new car. Demonstrators are usually only a few months old, are well equipped, have been properly serviced, and have had any problems ironed out. They also usually come with the balance of the manufacturer's warranty.

Doing your homework

Before you buy a new car, make sure that you know exactly what the 'on-road' price of the car should be, according to the manufacturer. The on-road price is:

- The price of the car itself, with any optional extras that you've chosen.
- The cost of registering the car for use on the road.
- The cost of making up and fitting number plates.
- Delivery charges.
- The cost of a year's road tax.

Often, the on-road price also includes a full tank of petrol.

Check to see exactly what's included in the price of the car. Often, items such as floor mats will be extra, although depending on the deal you manage to negotiate you may be able to persuade the dealer to 'throw them in.'

Depending on the type of new car you're hoping to buy, you may get a better deal during 'difficult' trading months, such as December and January, when the dealer is less likely to have a queue of customers lined up. Often, if you're interested in buying a car that a dealer already has in stock you'll be able to negotiate a better deal towards the end of a month – a dealer's sales figures and commissions for the sales staff are calculated at the end of each month, so if they've had a poor month they'll be keen to do a deal to improve their figures!

Check the press for the latest deals. Many manufacturers run special deals on certain models and these can be very competitive, often including in the price items that are normally optional extras, and sometimes a free year's insurance.

Doing the deal

When doing a deal to buy a new car, never instantly agree to pay the 'list' price – you should be able to negotiate a better deal. If you're buying a mainstream model, you should be able to negotiate a discount, and it's worth asking for prices from more than one dealer, so that you can compare what's on offer. If you're buying a prestige car, or a particularly popular model, you'll probably find it harder to negotiate a deal, as the dealer is likely to have a waiting list of customers who've placed orders for specific models. It's always going to be easier to negotiate a good deal on a car that a dealer has in stock than it is for a car that you have to order and then wait several months for.

If you have a car to trade in against a new car, make sure that you know what it's worth – it's rare for a dealer to give you a trade-in price equal to the market value of the car. If you don't mind the

extra work involved, it may pay to sell your existing car privately, as you'll probably get a better price for it, and you can then use this extra money towards your new car. When trading in, remember that the important price to consider is the 'price to trade up', not the price that the dealer offers you for your trade-in car. For instance, if one dealer offers you, say, £3,000 for your existing car, but no discount off the list price of a new car, and another dealer offers you £2,500 for your existing car and a £1,000 discount on the list price of the same new car, then the second deal is the best one, as you're £500 better off even though the dealer actually offered you less for your car.

Servicing

With a new car, it's important to note that in order to meet the warranty requirements you'll have to have the car serviced by an authorised dealer for the full period of the warranty. This can be expensive, as you'll have to pay dealer prices for servicing. Note that most manufacturers recommend that a new car is serviced after the first few hundred miles, just to check that all is well. You'll then be able to follow the normal service schedule.

BELOW Most main-dealer service departments provide a comfortable waiting area and slick service

Buying **used**

Buying a used car will obviously be cheaper than buying new and, for many people, is the only affordable way to own a car. Provided you do your homework, there's no reason why you shouldn't be able to find a well-looked-after, reliable car and negotiate a good deal, but it's important to be aware of the pitfalls waiting for the unwary. Never be afraid to ask for advice.

When buying a used car, the safest option is to buy from a recognised dealer. Riskier alternatives are to buy privately or at an auction. When buying any used car, bear in mind the following points.

- Don't buy the first car to catch your attention. If you've never driven the model of car you're thinking of buying, it's a good idea to view and drive several examples so that you can compare them.
- Don't be put off by high mileage. Most modern cars are capable of completing 100,000 miles or more without major problems, provided that they've been well maintained. A high mileage car that has been used mainly for motorway cruising may be in better shape than a low-mileage car which has been used for short journeys.
- Check the service history. The service book supplied with the car when new should have been completed and stamped by an authorised garage after each service. Cars with a full

service history ('fsh') usually command a higher price than those without. If the car is three years old or more, check that it has a new or very recent MoT certificate.

■ Don't view in the dark or wet. Water on the bodywork can give a misleading impression of the condition of the paintwork.

■ Check the indicated mileage, and ask yourself if it's genuine. If the car has covered a high mileage there will often be signs of wear on the driver's seat, in the driver's footwell around the pedals, and on the pedal rubbers.

■ Check for rust, and for signs of new or mismatched paint, which might show that the car has been involved in an accident. Check the tyres for signs of unusual wear or damage, and check that the car 'sits' evenly on its suspension, with all four corners at the same height.

■ Open the bonnet, and check for any obvious fluid leakage (oil, water, brake fluid), then start the engine and listen for any unusual noises. Also check for signs of excessive exhaust smoke. Blue smoke often indicates worn engine components, which may prove expensive to repair.

■ Check the locks. One key should operate all the locks and the ignition switch – if not, it's likely that the car has been broken into at some stage, and one or more of the locks has been replaced.

■ Drive the car, and test the brakes, steering, and gearbox. Make sure that the car doesn't pull to one side, and check that the steering feels positive and that the gears can be selected satisfactorily. Listen for any unusual noises or vibration, and keep an eye on the instruments and warning lights to make sure that they're working.

■ Don't be rushed into a deal. There will be plenty more cars to look at.

Vehicle inspections and vehicle history checks

Many of the motoring organisations offer a used car inspection service for a very reasonable fee. This involves a qualified engineer inspecting the car to make sure that there are no major faults or problems that are likely to cause trouble later. Be wary of a seller who refuses to let you have an inspection carried out – they probably have something to hide! If you decide not to have a vehicle inspection carried out, it's a good idea to take a knowledgeable friend with you to look at the car.

Even if you decide not to have a vehicle inspection carried out, it's very worthwhile considering a vehicle history check. Again, these checks on the background history of the car are offered by the major motoring organisations, and by several specialist companies. They usually include the following:

■ A check that the car has not been stolen.

■ A check that the car has not been written off by an insurance company at any point in its past.

■ A check to make sure that there is no finance outstanding on the car, and therefore that the car is not likely to be repossessed by a finance company.

■ A check on whether the registration number of the car has been changed at any point in the past.

■ A check on the recorded mileage, taken from registration document and MoT records.

■ A check on the VIN number and registration number against DVLA records.

■ A check on the recorded model details for the car, which will reveal whether that GTI you're looking at is really a GL in disguise!

These checks are extremely worthwhile, and most reputable companies providing this service include in their price a warranty against any of the checks proving to be incorrect.

BELOW A professional inspection can provide peace-of-mind when buying a used car

Paperwork

If you're buying a used car, especially from a dealer, make sure that it's been recently serviced. If it hasn't been, a dealer will normally service it for you before you take delivery – make sure that this is included in the price you've agreed to pay. Ask whether the car has a 'full service history'. A full service history should include a fully stamped service record book, to show that the car has been serviced in accordance with the manufacturer's recommendations, and you may find that the previous owner has also kept receipts for any work carried out. A car with a full service history is always worth more than an equivalent car without.

Similarly, always insist that the car is supplied with a 'new' MoT certificate, and if it isn't, negotiate a reduction in the price to compensate. Bear in mind that if the MoT certificate is due to expire shortly after you buy the car, you'll have to pay for the repairs necessary to correct any problems found during the test. A new MoT certificate provides you with peace of mind.

Check whether the car will be supplied with road tax, and if not, budget for taxing it. You must buy a tax disc before you can use a car on the road.

Ask to see the car's 'V5' Registration Document, and check that the details given on the document correspond to the vehicle you're thinking of buying. Check that the VIN number, the colour, and the description of the car correspond to the car you're looking at, and also check the number of 'previous keepers'. If the car has had a large number of owners, ask yourself why this might be – it could be that the car has had a troubled life!

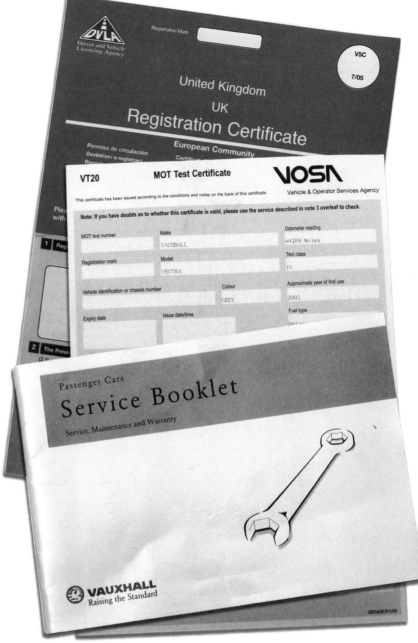

Prices

When you've decided on the particular model, or models, of car you're interested in buying, check the local papers, garage forecourts, and perhaps the specialist car sales papers and magazines to get an idea of the typical price such cars are selling for. Although there are plenty of websites and price guides that will give you some idea, the prices quoted are only approximate and can vary considerably from region to region. It may even be worth travelling away from your local area to get a better deal.

When comparing prices, make sure that you're comparing similar cars – for instance, a particular model of car may have had a 'facelift' or a new model may have been launched, but it may have the same registration letter as an example of the model that it superseded, which may explain a discrepancy in the prices of two apparently similar cars.

Prices should reflect the age, condition, recorded mileage and service history of a car – a low-mileage car with a full service history will normally be worth more than a similar car with higher mileage and/or an incomplete service history.

When viewing a car, check its condition carefully, and establish whether or not it's been serviced recently. If you notice any scratches, dents, or areas that have obviously been repaired, outside or inside the car, or if the car hasn't been serviced recently, negotiate a discount on the advertised price to allow for any work or servicing that needs to be done. Alternatively, make sure that the dealer is prepared to have the work done for you, at no extra charge, before agreeing to buy the car.

When it comes down to the final deal, provided a car's price isn't too far from the guide price that you've established, it's actually worth what you're prepared to pay for it. You're the customer, so if you're happy with the deal, that's all that really matters in the end.

Buying privately

If you've seen a private car advertised for sale, be aware that unscrupulous or 'amateur' trade sellers sometimes advertise cars as private sales. A trade seller is required by law to include a 'T' or the word 'Trade' in any advertisements for cars he or she is selling, no matter how small the ads may be. Not that there's anything wrong with buying a car from a small-time trader – it can actually be a good thing, as buying from a registered trader actually means that you have certain rights that you won't have if you buy from a private seller; for instance, a car sold by a dealer must be of 'satisfactory' quality, which means, amongst other things, that it must be free from defects – except ones that the dealer has pointed out to you and those which should have been found during a vehicle inspection (but only if an inspection has been carried out).

If you decide that you'd like to view a car, and you phone to make an appointment to see it, one way to catch out a trader who's posing as a private seller is to ask about 'the car you've advertised for sale', rather than asking about the specific model advertised. If the seller asks you which car, be wary, as it's unlikely that a private seller will have more than one car for sale. Ask

how long the seller has owned the car, and if they reply guardedly or say that they've only owned the car for a few months, the alarm bells should ring again. Take the initiative and ask if the seller is a private seller or a trader. If the seller is a trader, they've already broken the law by posing as a private seller in their advert, so their honesty is already questionable. Under such circumstances it would be advisable to walk away and cross that particular car off your list of 'possibles'.

Always ask to view the car at the seller's private address, and when you go to view it ask to see the 'V5' Registration Document, and check that the address appearing corresponds to the address at which you're viewing the car – if not, ask the seller why.

Ask to see the service receipts and MoT test certificates. This will help to establish that the car has been properly looked after, that it hasn't been stolen, and that the recorded mileage is genuine.

There are some genuine bargains to be had by buying privately, so don't be put off. Provided you do your homework and take all the obvious precautions, you'll usually manage to negotiate a better deal privately than you will with a dealer.

ABOVE When buying privately, the ability to pay cash be a useful bargaining tool

OPPOSITE ABOVE When buying a used car, always ask to see the Registration Document, MoT Certificate and service record

OPPOSITE BELOW There are a number of magazines and guides providing advice on buying a used car

ABOVE Franchised
dealers usually have
a good selection of
low-mileage used
cars for sale

Buying from a dealer

Though you'll generally pay more for a car bought
from a dealer's forecourt than you will for a car
purchased privately, you will at least have the
peace of mind that you have certain rights when
you buy from a dealer – if something goes wrong
with the car shortly after you buy it, you have
some chance of sorting it out if you've bought
from a dealer, whereas if you buy privately you
have no rights.

If you've been watching the adverts in your
local area for a while, bear in mind that if a dealer
has had a car sitting on his forecourt for a few
weeks he'll be more willing to do a deal on it than
he will on a car that has only just arrived.

Most dealers will advertise a used car for sale
at a price that will allow them to be 'knocked
down' by a potential buyer, so never instantly offer
to pay the advertised price unless the car is a
particularly rare or desirable model.

Check exactly what's included in the price.
Is a warranty included (refer to the advice on
warranties earlier in this chapter), is road tax
included, and will the car have a service and a
new MoT certificate when you take delivery? If
the answer to any of these questions is no,
negotiate a discount on the price to allow for
the costs involved. Be wary of a car being sold

without a new, or at least a recent, MoT – if you
subsequently take the car for an MoT yourself and
problems are discovered, you'll have to pay to get
them fixed, and in the worst cases you could be
faced with a hefty bill.

Before you go along to view a car, set yourself a
price limit. Don't exceed your limit, and don't tell
the dealer what your limit is! If you walk away from
a deal because the dealer wants a little more than
you can afford, ask him to think about it, and if the
dealer has little interest from other potential buyers
you may get a phone call a few days later asking if
you're still interested in doing a deal!

Buying from an auction

Car auctions can be intimidating for the uninitiated,
but there are some genuine bargains to be found,
and most dealers buy a good proportion of their
stock from auctions. Unless there are an unusual
number of private bidders present, a car sold at
auction will go for very close to its trade value,
which will be significantly lower than its retail value.
Auctions can also provide nasty shocks for the
unwary, as it's possible for a seller to get a quick
sale with little or no comeback.

There are various different types of auctions,
and some are much safer for an inexperienced
buyer than others. 'Manufacturer' and 'Fleet' sales

probably provide the best chance of a good buy for a first-time buyer. These sales often include low-mileage cars, with warranted mileage and a full or part service history. A fleet car has usually been looked after and serviced in accordance with the manufacturer's recommendations, and you may even find that the car is supplied with a full print-out detailing all the servicing that has been carried out.

'Fleet and Finance' sales often include a mix of fleet cars and repossessed vehicles being sold by finance houses. Such sales can provide bargains, especially if they include almost-new stock from a recently bankrupted dealer, but they can also include less desirable cars.

'General' sales comprise all kinds of cars, including those being sold by private individuals. Again, you'll find bargains in a general sale, but also a fair proportion of less desirable cars.

Other types of auctions include 'Part Exchange' sales, where you'll often find older cars which a franchised dealer doesn't want to put on his forecourt, and 'themed' sales, such as 'Late Year, Low Mileage', '4x4s', and 'Diesel Cars', in which most of the cars are usually being sold by dealers – be wary! There are also

'Classic Car' sales, which are generally aimed at the private buyer.

When buying at auction, it pays to visit an auction before the day on which you intend to buy, just to get a feel for how things work. Cars for sale will have a sticker on the windscreen showing the lot number, and will be lined up, often very close together, outside the auction halls. Just before each car is due to be sold, it will be started up and driven into the auction hall. The auctioneer will then give a brief description of the car and of any paperwork and history that comes with it, before bidding starts. Bidders in the hall will signal that they are bidding, usually by raising an arm, although seasoned traders may use much more subtle signals. When a bidder has reached his maximum bid, and wishes to stop bidding he will usually shake his head to signify that he doesn't wish to bid further. The auctioneer will invite any further bids, and if none are forthcoming the hammer will fall and the car is sold. The car will then be driven out of the auction hall to a secure compound. This whole process usually takes less than a minute.

Most reputable auction houses produce a guide for first-time auction goers, and some also

BELOW When attending a vehicle auction, always buy a catalogue for the sales you're interested in

ABOVE Try to watch a number of cars going through the auction halls to get a feel for how things work

have very good websites that enable you to view or download catalogues for forthcoming auctions.

Bear in mind that if you buy a car at an auction you'll normally have to pay a buyer's fee, in addition to the purchase price of the car. The buyer's fee can vary from under a hundred pounds to several hundred, depending on the selling price of the car. Also, check on the methods of payment accepted by the auction house – few will accept credit cards, and if you pay by cheque you won't be able to take the car away until the cheque has cleared. You'll also probably have to pay a cash deposit of a few hundred pounds immediately after placing a winning bid.

Here are a few tips for buying at auction:

- Set yourself a price limit, and don't bid above it.
- Buy a catalogue for the auctions you're interested in, which will provide details of all the cars for sale, and will also give times for the sales.
- Try to watch a number of cars going through the auction halls before you intend to bid. Each auctioneer has his own style, and it can take a while to 'tune in' to the language and phrases being used, and to recognise the signals for placing bids.
- Take a good look at any car you're interested in before it reaches the auction hall, and try to be around when the car is started up, so that you can check for smoke or unusual noises.

- If possible watch a few similar cars going through the auction, so that you know roughly how much a particular model is selling for on the day.
- Check whether a car is being sold with paperwork, MoT, or tax, and check whether the mileage declared is warranted as genuine.
- Some cars are sold with a guarantee of 'no major mechanical faults' while others are 'sold as seen'. In either case, you normally have an hour from the fall of the hammer to report any major problems and try to seek an amicable solution. With 'sold as seen' cars there is rarely anything you can do if you find a problem.
- With reputable auction houses, the buyer's premium will usually include a warranty that the car has not been stolen, is not a write-off, and has no outstanding finance on it, which could mean that it might yet be seized by a finance company.
- You assume ownership of the car from the moment the hammer falls on your winning bid, and therefore you should insure it as quickly as possible thereafter – if the car is damaged on the auction site after you've bought it, there's very little you can do unless you've insured it.
- If you intend to drive your new car home after the auction, make sure that it's taxed, and that you either have a can of petrol with you or know where the nearest garage is – most cars are sold with very little petrol in the tank!

Selling a car

If you're going to sell your car, the first thing to do is to decide what price to ask. Various price guides are available, and some magazines provide price guides for second-hand cars. It also pays to look in the local papers, and on local garage forecourts, to see what prices are being asked for similar models to yours. The price you can expect depends on the car's age, condition, and mileage. Don't ask too much, but it's a good idea to ask for more than you're hoping to sell the car for – then there's some room for negotiation between you and the buyer.

Once you've decided on how much to ask for your car, you need to advertise it. Most local papers and magazines carry advertisements for a reasonable cost, but if you want to reach a more specific audience it's worth placing an advert in one of the specialist car sales papers or magazines.

Think about the wording of your advert. You need to give as much positive information as possible, without using too many words. Give details of the model and engine size, service history (where applicable), colour, age, mileage, condition, and any desirable options or equipment. If you've owned the car from new, it's always worth stating 'one owner'.

Bear in mind the points that the prospective buyer will be looking for. It goes without saying that the car should be clean and tidy, as first impressions are important. Any fluid leaks should be cured, and there's no point in trying to disguise any major bodywork or mechanical problems.

Before you invite any prospective buyers to view the car, remove any extras that you've fitted which you want to keep (such as in-car entertainment equipment), or at least tell any prospective purchasers that you intend to remove such equipment and that it's not included in the sale.

Make sure that the service documents, registration document, etc, are available for inspection. If the existing MoT test certificate has only a few months to run, have the car tested so that it has a new certificate, if you can do so without too much expense – it will make the car much more saleable.

You're likely to sell your car more quickly and get a better price if you sell at the right time of year. It's always best to sell in the spring or summer rather than in the winter.

Don't allow the buyer to take the car away until you have their money, and it's a good idea to ask them to sign a piece of paper to say that they're happy to buy the car as viewed, just in case any problems develop later on. Give a receipt for the money paid.

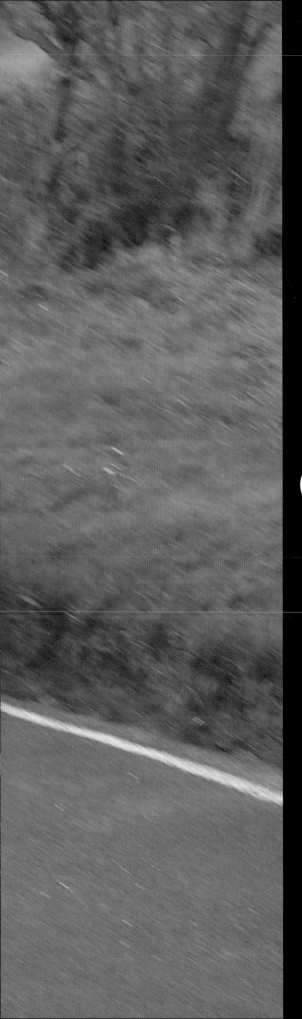

Getting on the road

Learning
to drive

Learning to drive is a big step in most people's lives, and can be a ticket to independence. Sitting behind the wheel of a car for the first time can be daunting, even though you'll almost certainly have travelled as a passenger countless times, but plenty of practice and determination will pay off and will make it all the more rewarding when you pass your test and throw away the L-plates!

For a complete all-in-one guide to learning to drive, including sample theory test questions, refer to *Learn to Drive*, also published by Haynes Publishing.

The law for learners

Before you can learn to drive, however, there are a few essential things that you need to take care of. In the UK, the law states that to drive a car on public roads as a learner driver, you must:

- Be at least 17 years old (except if you're receiving the highest rate of mobility allowance, in which case you can start learning at 16)
- Hold a provisional driving licence

- Be covered by a suitable car insurance policy
- Be supervised by a driver who is at least 21 years old, and has held a full driving licence for at least three years
- Ensure that the car you're driving is roadworthy, taxed, and has a current MoT certificate (if it's over three years old)
- Display L-plates on the front and rear of the car
- Not drive on motorways

Driving lessons

You may have a member of your family or a friend who's willing to supervise you when you're learning to drive, but there's no substitute for proper lessons with an Approved Driving Instructor (ADI). Although, from a cost point of view, sticking with a friend or family member may seem an attractive option, they're unlikely to have the valuable experience of teaching that an ADI has to call on and, more importantly, they may never have experienced the current driving test themselves.

The ideal approach to learning to drive is to start out with an instructor, then once they're happy that you've gained enough confidence to master the basics, you can think about having extra practice with a relative or friend sitting alongside you. If you do decide to learn with a relative or friend, it's a very wise investment to have at least a few lessons with an ADI before your test, just to make sure that you're aware of what's involved, and that you're familiar with what the examiner's going to ask you to do during the test.

There's no substitute for practice when preparing to take the driving test, and the more miles you cover the better. Try to practice on as many different types of road as possible, and once your confidence has built up don't be shy of driving in busy traffic – the greater the number of different situations you've experienced, the less likely you are to be caught out by an unfamiliar situation during your test.

Choosing an instructor

Approved Driving Instructors have to be registered with the Driving Standards Agency (DSA) and by law they have to have an ADI qualification – which involves taking a rigorous driving test and regular assessments – to be able to accept money in return for providing driving lessons. ADIs are graded, and need to have achieved at least Grade 4 to be considered competent, whilst Grade 5 is good and Grade 6 is a very high standard. Note that trainee driving instructors are allowed to give driving lessons before they qualify as ADIs – trainee instructors normally display a triangular pink certificate on their car's windscreen, whilst qualified ADIs usually display a hexagonal green certificate.

BELOW Learning to drive can be fun, and for many new drivers can provide a big step towards independence

RIGHT Trainee driving instructors may display a pink certificate (left), while qualified instructors display a green certificate (right)

Driving Standards Agency

Licence No. **164606**

Licensed Trainee

Driving Instructor (Car)

Certificate No.

293394

Driving Standards Agency

Expires

Approved Driving Instructor (car)

BELOW Driving in traffic may seem daunting at first, but will soon become second nature

Don't overlook the fact that you also need to consider whether or not you're going to be able to get along with your instructor – whilst you don't have to be best friends, having the best-qualified instructor in the country isn't going to help if you really don't like each other! Word of mouth is a good guide to an instructor's record, and a recommendation from a relative or friend who's recently learnt to drive is a good starting point.

The driving test

The driving test, which you must pass before you can gain a full licence and drive solo, has two parts – a theory part and a practical part. You must pass the theory test before you can take the practical test, and you must take the practical test within two years of passing the theory test. Although there are two separate parts to the test, and both must be passed

DRIVING STANDARDS AGENCY
DRIVING TEST CENTRE

before you qualify for a full licence, the two parts go hand in hand, and there's no need to pass the theory test before you learn to drive – in fact, the points covered by the theory test will make much more sense if you're already learning to drive, and have some experience on the road.

The theory test is split into two parts, and includes a multiple-choice test which takes around 40 minutes using a touch-screen, and a hazard perception test which takes around half an hour and is based on video clips.

The practical test lasts around 40 minutes, and involves driving with an examiner in the passenger seat, who will instruct you on what route to take and will assess your driving. During the test the examiner will check your eyesight by asking you to read a car number plate, and will ask you to perform several set manoeuvres. You'll also be asked questions about car safety checks.

Further details of the driving test can be obtained from the Driving Standards Agency (DSA). The contact details are given in Appendix C.

The Pass Plus scheme

The Pass Plus scheme is designed to help newly qualified drivers improve their skills, and is supported by the DSA and by insurers, who may offer cheaper insurance to drivers who have taken the Pass Plus course. Anyone who has a full licence can take part in the scheme.

The course consists of six training sessions designed to follow on from the standard driving test. Each session lasts for about an hour, and the sessions cover driving:

■ In town
■ On rural roads
■ In all weathers
■ At night
■ On dual carriageways
■ On motorways

There's no test to take during the course, but drivers are continually assessed during each session and, assuming that they successfully complete each of the six sessions, a certificate is awarded at the end of the course.

Enrolling in the Pass Plus scheme is well worth considering, as it will help you become a safer and better driver, and you'll gain extra driving experience to help you deal with situations you may never have come across whilst learning to drive. You could also save more than the cost of the course on your insurance premium. The DSA will be able to provide a list of insurers who give discounts to holders of Pass Plus certificates.

ABOVE Once you've passed the theory and practical parts of the driving test, you can take off those L-plates!

Paperwork

Once you have a Driving Licence, if you have the use of your own car there's additional paperwork that you'll need to obtain and keep safe.

As a driver, by law you must have:
- A Driving Licence
- A valid Certificate of Insurance

If you own a car, by law you must have for the car:
- A Vehicle Registration Document
- A tax disc
- An MoT certificate (if the car is more than three years old)

You must keep all this paperwork safe, and you may be asked to produce certain paperwork if you're involved in an accident, or if the police stop you for any reason. It's a good idea to carry your driving licence with you at all times, and you must display a valid tax disc on the car at all times, but the other paperwork is best kept safely at home – don't be tempted to keep it in your car, as this will provide all that a car thief needs for an easy life, and if your car is involved in an accident or a fire the paperwork may be lost.

Driving Licence

If you're planning to learn to drive, you'll first need to obtain a Provisional Driving Licence. Driving Licences are issued by the Driver and Vehicle Licensing

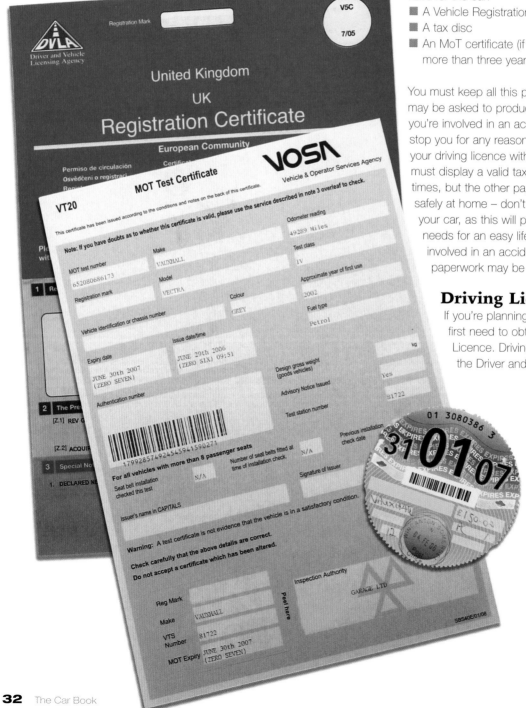

LEFT A full driving licence allows you to legally drive on your own, unsupervised

Agency (DVLA – see Appendix C for address details), and you'll need to apply for a provisional licence using form D1, which is available from most post offices. Once you've signed your provisional licence you're entitled to drive on a public road, as long as you're supervised by a driver sitting in the car with you at all times who holds a full licence. It's illegal to drive 'solo' on a provisional licence. Once you've passed both the theory and practical parts of the driving test, you can apply for a full driving licence, and you're then legally able to drive on your own, unsupervised.

Bear in mind that you can learn to drive using a car with a manual or an automatic gearbox, but if you learn and take your practical test in an automatic car your full licence will only allow you to drive an automatic, and you won't legally be able to drive a car with a manual gearbox. If you learn to drive in a car with a manual gearbox you'll be able to drive both manual and automatic cars once you've passed your test.

Insurance certificate

When you insure your car, you'll be issued with a Certificate of Insurance to prove that you're insured. The details shown on the certificate vary depending on the insurance company that issued it, but as a minimum it will show your name and address, the car's registration number, the date of issue of the certificate and the date it expires, along with details of the insurance company, and details of the type of insurance policy you have.

Always keep your insurance certificate in a safe place, as it's an important legal document and you'll need it when you tax your car. You may also need to refer to it if you're unfortunate enough to be involved in an accident.

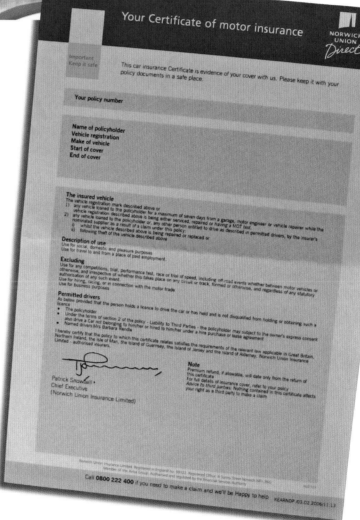

When your insurance company issues a Certificate of Insurance you'll usually also receive a Policy Schedule, which lays down the terms of the insurance, and explains what's covered by the policy and what isn't. Make sure that you keep this safe too, as you'll almost certainly need to refer to it if you need to make a claim.

ABOVE Whenever you receive a new insurance certificate, always check that all the details shown are correct

Vehicle Registration Document ('V5')

By law, every vehicle must have a Vehicle Registration Document, and you should keep it safe, as you'll need it if you sell or scrap the car, and you may need it to buy a tax disc.

The Registration Document – known as a 'V5' – shows the registered keeper of the vehicle. The keeper is the person who keeps the vehicle on a public road, and is not always necessarily the legal owner of the vehicle. The document gives the keeper's name and address and the registration number of the vehicle. It also gives other information about the vehicle, such as the date it was first registered, the Vehicle Identification Number (VIN), engine number, colour, engine size, body type, etc. The number of previous keepers is usually shown too. The form also includes sections that must be filled in when a vehicle is sold, both by the buyer and by the seller, who must notify the DVLA of the change of ownership (see Chapter 1 for more details).

Tax disc

All cars registered in the UK must display a tax disc (the official term is a Vehicle Excise Licence) on the left-hand side of the windscreen, which shows that the owner has paid the vehicle's 'excise duty'.

You can buy a disc to last for six or twelve months. To obtain one, you'll need to present your insurance certificate and the car's MoT certificate, and if you haven't been sent a renewal notice in the post you may also need to show the car's Registration Document.

For cars registered before 1 March 2001, the rate of tax depends on the engine size – cars with an engine up to 1,549cc are eligible for a cheaper rate. For cars registered after 1 March 2001, the rate depends on the level of carbon dioxide (CO_2) emissions – the less CO_2 the engine produces, the lower the tax rate.

It's worth noting that cars built (not necessarily registered) before 1st January 1973 are considered to be 'classics' and there's no charge for a tax disc, although a tax disc must still be displayed.

BELOW Besides an insurance certificate, the three must-have documents you need to keep you car legal are a Registration Document, and MoT certiicate and a tax disc

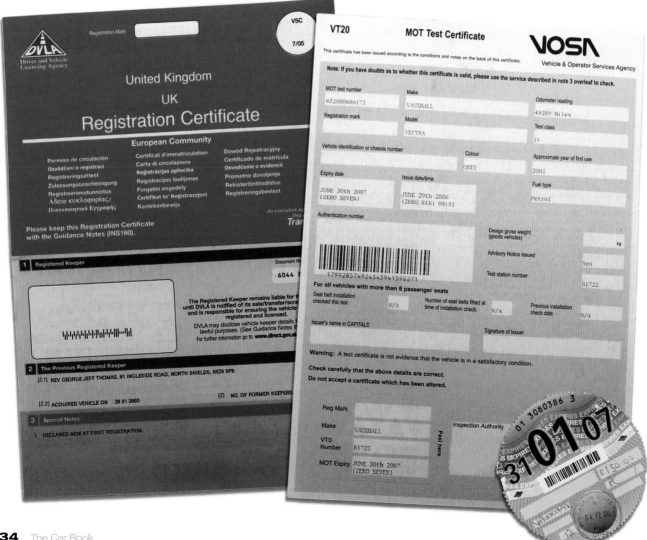

Service Record

1st Service	2nd Service	3rd Service	4th Service
After one year or 20 000 miles/30 000 km after delivery	After one year or 20 000 miles/30 000 km after previous service	After one year or 20 000 miles/30 000 km after previous service	After one year or 20 000 miles/30 000 after previous service
Date **29.07.03**	Date **3.8.04**	Date	Date
Miles/km **12203**	Miles/km **26985**	Miles/km	Miles/km

Engine oil change

	1st Service	2nd Service	3rd Service	4th Service
Oil grade ACEA - A3-98/B3-98				
Oil viscosity[1] W-				

Yes No Change of
- Battery for remote control
- Brake fluid
- Spark plugs
- Air cleaner element
- Fuel filter
- Pollen filter
- Toothed belt + tensioning pulley

(1st Service stamp) DAVISONS OF MORPETH 01670 512115

(2nd Service) GBC630 / CD Bramall York / Vauxhall / Malton Road / York / YO32 9TE / Tel: 01904 426688

Vauxhall Dealer's Stamp and Signature

Next Service:
Date _____ Miles/km _____

Whichever occurs first.

1) Only SAE 0W-X, 5W-X or 10W-X (X min. 30)

12

MoT certificate

All cars need an MoT certificate when they're three years old, and you'll need to present the MoT certificate when you buy a tax disc. An MoT certificate expires after 12 months, so once a car is three years old it must have an MoT test every year.

The MoT certificate is issued after the car has passed an MoT test, which consists of a number of checks to make sure that a car is roadworthy and that its exhaust emissions are within the legal limits. MoT tests can only be carried out at an official MoT Testing Station – not all garages can carry out MoT tests, but the ones that do usually advertise the service and often display an official sign outside showing that they are authorised to carry out the test.

You can have your car tested up to one month before the current certificate runs out – the expiry date of the new certificate will be 12 months after the date of expiry of the old one.

The MoT certificate shows details of the car, including the registration number, VIN number, and the mileage recorded when the test was carried out, and the date of issue and expiry of the certificate.

It's worth making a note in your diary of the date when your car's MoT is due, as a reminder to book it in for a test. It's illegal to drive a car on the road if the MoT certificate has expired.

It's a good idea to keep all the old MoT certificates, as when you come to sell the car the certificates will help to prove that the car's mileage is genuine.

Refer to 'Preparing for an MoT test' on page 158 for more details.

Service records

When a car is new, it comes with a service record book which shows details of all the scheduled servicing recommended by the manufacturer. Spaces are provided so that the garage carrying out servicing can stamp the book and write in the mileage and date. Although there's no requirement to keep this book, or even to have it stamped, it does provide a record to prove that the car has been serviced in line with the manufacturer's recommended schedule. This can be very useful when you're buying or selling a car, because as long as the service record book contains the official stamps of the garages that carried out the servicing it shows that the car has been properly serviced. Cars with a 'full service history' tend to sell for a better price than those without.

Some owners keep all the invoices and receipts for servicing, and these can be useful when you sell the car as they provide more evidence that it has been looked after.

ABOVE An up-to-date service record will prove a big plus when it comes to selling your car

Insurance

It's a legal requirement to insure your car before you drive on the road, and insuring a car for the first time can be an expensive business.

Taking out an insurance policy for the first time

Although it's possible for young drivers to save money by adding their name to a parent's insurance policy, in the long term this can prove to be an expensive option, because the sooner a driver takes out an insurance policy in their own name the sooner they will start to build up a no-claims discount (assuming that no claims are made). Building up no-claims discount can make a significant difference to the premium – most insurance companies give maximum no-claims discount after around five or six years, which equates to a discount of around 60–65 per cent.

LEFT When shopping around for insurance on the 'phone, make sure that you have all your details to hand

Choosing the level of cover

There are three basic levels of cover offered by insurance companies, although there are really only two that should be considered unless you're on an extremely tight budget. The levels of cover are generally as follows, but every policy varies slightly, so check exactly what's covered by the policy before you buy:

■ Fully comprehensive cover will provide you with full cover for any damage to your car, even if you back into a gatepost, will provide you with cover against damaging other people's vehicles or property, and will also cover your car if it catches fire or is stolen.
■ Third party, fire and theft (TPFT) cover will provide you with cover against damaging other people's vehicles or property, and will also cover your car if it catches fire or is stolen. However, TPFT cover will not cover you if you accidentally damage your own car.
■ The remaining option is 'third party only' (TP) cover, which is really only worth considering if you have a very cheap car. It will only cover you for damage to other people's cars and property, and you won't be covered if your car is stolen or catches fire. This option is really only a last resort, and many insurance companies no longer offer TP cover.

Fully comprehensive insurance costs more than other types of policy, but bear in mind that the cost of repairing accident damage on a modern car can be very high.

Although your policy will usually provide you with cover to meet the minimum legal requirements when driving in other EC countries, you may have to pay an additional premium if you want the same level of cover there that you enjoy at home.

When taking out an insurance policy you may be asked if you want 'legal protection', and sometimes this is included automatically with your policy. This service is worth having, as it will help to pay for legal action to recover any costs that you may have to pay in the case of an accident that wasn't your fault. Insurance companies may also be able to offer you discounted membership of one of the motoring assistance organisations as part of an insurance policy package.

It really is up to the individual to choose the best policy to suit their needs, but fully comprehensive cover has to be the best bet if you can afford it.

Getting the best quote

It's always worth shopping around for insurance quotes, because they can vary enormously. Insurance is big business, and there are specialist companies who offer good rates to drivers above a certain age, drivers with a poor driving record, etc. There are also many insurance brokers, who will shop around for the best deal on your behalf – but bear in mind that they take a commission

Reducing insurance premiums

The best way to save money on insurance is to keep your driving record clean, and shop around when the insurance is due for renewal, but there are other steps that can be taken to reduce the bill.

- Insurance costs are higher for young and/or inexperienced drivers, so by restricting the cover to older experienced drivers the premium will be reduced.
- If your car doesn't cover very many miles, you can reduce your premium by restricting the annual mileage.
- The premium can often be reduced significantly by increasing your voluntary excess. The excess is the contribution that you must pay towards the cost of any repair, which can vary from a few pounds to several hundreds. Increasing the excess means that you'll have to pay more if you make a claim, but your annual premium will be lower.
- Restricting the level of cover can also make savings. It may not be worth insuring an older car with comprehensive cover.
- Some insurance companies will give a discount to members of motoring clubs, especially 'one-make' clubs, who can often negotiate worthwhile savings for their members.
- If your car doesn't have a standard-fitment security system, fitting an approved immobiliser or alarm system is likely to reduce your premium.

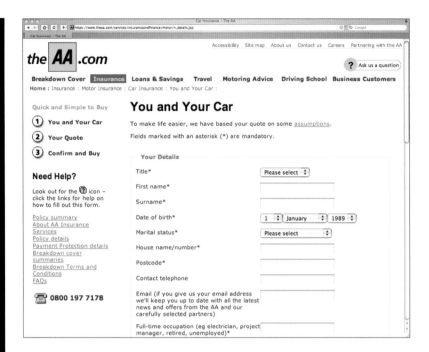

ABOVE Most of the major insurance companies have websites that enable you to fill in a proposal form and obtain a quote on-line

LEFT Fitting a car security system will help to deter thieves – it's worth paying to have a system professionally fitted

on each policy they sell, so although you should receive an expert personnel service you may not get the best deal.

Almost all of the big insurance companies will provide quotes direct, either over the phone or via the internet. Most of the major insurance companies provide an internet service which allows you to obtain quotes and take out a policy on-line. The advantage of this is that companies usually offer a discount – sometimes as much as 20 per cent – for buying a policy on-line. If you run into any problems when taking out a policy on-line, or if the options provided don't enable you to provide all the required information truthfully, it's best to abort and phone the company to clarify things – if you tell the assistant that you were trying to take out a policy on-line they'll probably still give you the on-line discount.

It's always worth shopping around for quotes from different companies, but make sure that the policies you're comparing are similar. Often policies differ in detail – for instance, many policies provide windscreen cover without affecting your no-claims bonus, and you may have the use of a courtesy car whilst your own is being repaired. Many of the larger insurance companies deal with their own approved repairers, so if you need to have damage repaired you won't have to take your car to several different garages to obtain quotes for repair prices. You may also find that the insurance company will arrange for your car to be picked up and delivered back to you when the repairs are complete.

LEFT If you're unfortunate enough to have an accident, most large insurance companies will arrange for your car to be repaired quickly by an approved repairer

No-claims discount

Every year that you're insured without making a claim, your insurer gives you a discount, up to a maximum of around 60–65 per cent after five or six years. If you make a claim, you lose one or two years' worth of discount, so think about whether it's worth putting in a claim to cover the cost of repairing minor damage, especially if you have to pay an excess.

Some companies offer 'no-claims discount protection' for an extra fee. Read the small print carefully before deciding whether this option is worthwhile.

What information will the insurance company need?

Always be totally truthful when you answer the insurance company's questions, and if you're in any doubt as to whether a piece of information is relevant, tell them anyway. If you need to make a claim, and there's something important that you forgot to state when taking out your policy, the insurance company may not pay out.

Although some insurance companies may ask for additional information, most of them will ask for the following:

- Your name, address and postcode.
- The names of any other drivers who will drive the car.
- The dates of birth of all drivers including yourself.
- The occupations of all drivers including yourself.

- Details of any accidents that you or any of the drivers have had in the last few years.
- Details of any recent motoring offences or convictions for any of the drivers.
- The make, model, and registration number of the car.
- The car's current value.
- Details of any modifications from the car's standard specification.
- Whether or not you'll be using the car in connection with your work.
- Where you'll be parking the car overnight (garage, driveway, or street).
- What sort of cover you require.

Making a claim

Read your policy document so that you know what to do if you have to make a claim. If you're involved in an accident, or if your car suffers damage, inform your insurance company as soon as possible. You'll have to fill in a claim form, giving details of exactly what happened. Make sure that you give as much information as possible, and if you're involved in an accident try to obtain the name and address of an independent witness.

It's important to provide as much detail as possible when making a claim, but always be truthful. Also bear in mind that if you admit responsibility for an accident at the scene, it will be difficult to change your mind later!

In some cases it can take a long time for an insurance claim to be settled, particularly if there is a dispute about who was to blame.

Breakdown organisations

A breakdown can prove to be expensive if you find yourself stranded at the roadside. Garage recovery charges can be very high, especially if you suffer a breakdown on a motorway. If you have to call out a recovery vehicle, you'll almost certainly find that the call-out charge will be more than the cost of a year's membership of one of the breakdown organisations. If you're not a member of a breakdown organisation, a local garage will usually only recover your car to their premises, in which case you'll still have to pay to get your car fixed. If your car can't be fixed quickly, you'll be stranded without transport.

You'll find that there are a number of packages available from the various motoring organisations, and you should be able to find one that suits your requirements. Some will guarantee to take your car and passengers to your home or to your destination, whichever suits you best, whilst others may only transport your car to the nearest garage. You may also be able to choose an option which will provide assistance if you have trouble starting your car at home, and some packages will provide full cover if you take your car abroad.

Your insurance company may offer annual membership of one of the motoring organisations at a discounted rate, which may be worth considering, and membership of a motoring or motorsport club often entitles you to a discount. Many new cars come with free membership of one of the motoring organisations for the first year of ownership, or sometimes longer.

Obtain information from several breakdown organisations, and read everything carefully before deciding which package is most suitable. Always check carefully to see what's included, and make sure that you're aware of any limits on the cover – occasionally, there's a limit on the age of the car that can be covered, or there may be an extra charge for older cars.

The larger motoring organisations, such as the AA and the RAC, offer a range of additional

LEFT The majority of breakdown call-outs result in the problem being fixed at the roadside

benefits and discounts to members, such as route-planning services, and a vehicle inspection service that will provide a report on the condition of any car that you may be thinking of buying. Think of membership of a breakdown organisation as a second insurance policy – you're buying the peace of mind that goes with knowing that assistance is never far away should the worst happen.

LEFT It's comforting to know that help is never far away, even in the worst of conditions

Using
your car

Gadgets
and tool kits

It's a good idea to keep a few items in your boot to get you out of trouble if you have a problem during a journey. In fact it's worth noting that in some countries it's actually compulsory to carry certain items, such as a warning triangle, first aid kit, and spare light bulbs. The basic tool kit supplied with your car won't allow you to do much more than change a wheel, so it's a good idea to carry a few extra basic tools just in case. Even if you can't fix a problem yourself, someone else might be able to if you can supply a screwdriver!

Emergency kit and spares

Here's a selection of items and spares which you might want to carry – the list could be endless, but it's a case of striking a balance between taking up too much space in your boot and having the necessary item to get you out of trouble.

▲ Warning triangle

▲ Wheel brace with extending handle

▲ Spare bulbs and fuses

▲ First aid kit
Fire extinguisher ▶

▲ Windscreen de-icer spray (in winter)

▲ Ice scraper (in winter)

▲ Spare alternator drivebelt

▲ Coil of stout wire

▲ Selection of cable ties

▲ Roll of insulating tape

▲ Selection of hose clips

◀ Can of water-dispersant spray (such as WD-40)

Luggage restraints ▶ (elastic 'bungee' type)

Tools

Here are some tools that won't take up much space and might help to fix simple problems at the roadside. If you decide to carry out DIY maintenance, you'll need these tools anyway.

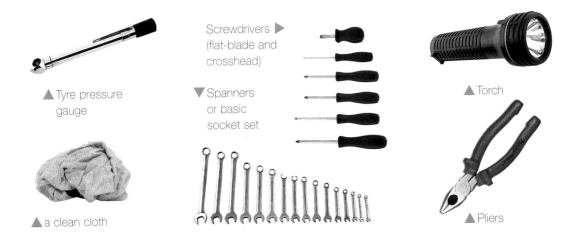

▲ Tyre pressure gauge

Screwdrivers ▶ (flat-blade and crosshead)

▼ Spanners or basic socket set

▲ Torch

▲ a clean cloth

▲ Pliers

Car security

Car manufacturers are far more aware of car security these days, and most new cars are supplied with etched window glass, immobilisers, alarms, and protected in-car entertainment equipment as standard.

Simple security measures

Apart from using security devices, there are several common-sense steps you can take to make life harder for would-be criminals. Some of the points might seem obvious, but in the majority of car crime cases the car is broken into or stolen in a very short space of time, with little force or effort required.

■ Always lock your car – even in the garage or driveway at home, or if you've just filled up with fuel and are popping into the kiosk to pay. Many modern cars have anti-theft deadlocks – if your car has them, make sure you always activate them when locking your car. Don't forget to lock the fuel filler (if it has a separate lock), and if the car's in the garage, lock the garage. If your car is stolen or broken into while it's unlocked, your insurance company may not pay out.

- Always remove the ignition key – even in the garage or driveway at home.
- Close all the windows and the sunroof – if a window or sunroof is open, you're making a criminal's job much easier. A door can be opened much more quickly with the aid of an open window.
- Park in a visible location – if possible, always try to park in an attended car park, and in a space where your car's highly visible. If you have to park at night, in a car park or at the roadside, try to pick a well-lit area (under a street light for instance).
- Never leave valuable items on display – if you can't take it with you, lock it in the boot. Don't leave valuable items in the glovebox. Don't leave your vehicle documents in the car, as they could help a thief to sell it.
- If your car has a telescopic radio aerial, put it down when parking – alternatively, you can have a telescopic aerial replaced with a less vulnerable flexible rubber one.
- Protect in-car entertainment (ICE) equipment – most modern equipment is security-coded, and won't work if it's disconnected from the battery. If your ICE equipment has a removable panel, make sure you remove it when you leave the car.

ABOVE Don't say that you haven't been warned – signs like this shouldn't be ignored!

BELOW Locking wheel nuts will help to protect against the theft of expensive alloy wheels

Security equipment

Most modern cars have immobilisers and alarm systems as standard equipment, and many also have the glass etched with the registration number or VIN number. If your car has an alarm or immobiliser, make sure that you use it! It's worth noting that most insurance companies give a discount for cars fitted with an immobiliser and/or alarm system.

If your car doesn't have any security equipment, think about fitting some or all of the following. There's a wide range of equipment available to suit most budgets:

- Consider having an immobiliser fitted – electronic immobilisers will prevent the engine from being started, and mechanical devices such as steering wheel and gear-lever locks can act as a visible deterrent.
- Consider having an alarm fitted – the best alarms are expensive, but they will deter thieves. Many alarms have built in immobilisers, and it's even possible to fit a tracking system that will allow the police to monitor the movement of a stolen car. Fitting an alarm system can be a tricky job, as it means tapping in to the car's electrical system, so it's wise to have it professionally fitted.
- Have your car windows etched with the registration number or Vehicle Identification Number – this will help to trace your car if it's stolen and the thieves try to change its identity. Other glass components such as sunroofs and headlights can also be etched. Many garages and windscreen specialists can provide this service.
- Use locking wheel nuts – if your car has expensive alloy wheels, always use locking wheel nuts to deter thieves. Alloy wheels are the first item on many thieves' shopping lists!

Load carrying

Occasionally, you may want to use your car to carry a heavy or unusual load, or leisure equipment such as cycles or skis, and a large range of load-carrying equipment is available to suit almost every need.

Roof bars and racks

In the past, roof racks were generally the main method of carrying luggage on the roof of a car. Since roof bars and roof boxes became more widespread, fewer people use roof racks and fewer accessory shops stock them, but you may still opt to use a roof rack for unusual loads, or if security isn't a problem.

Some roof bars and racks claim to be 'universal', while others are tailor-made for a particular model of car. On some cars, you may have no option but to use the manufacturer's own roof rails or rack.

Many manufacturers produce complete luggage carrying systems, with roof bars and compatible luggage trays, cycle carriers, etc. Often, you can buy a basic set of roof bars with a separate mounting adapter kit to fit your car. This means you'll still be able to use the bars if you change your car – you just buy the appropriate adapter kit.

Using a roof rack

If you're going to use a roof rack, first make sure that it's correctly fitted to the car – follow the manufacturer's instructions. Next, you need to make sure that you load the rack sensibly. You'll usually find a maximum roof rack load specified in your car's handbook – don't exceed it!

Before you put anything on the roof rack, spread a large sheet of plastic or a tarpaulin over the rack (make sure that it's big enough to wrap completely around the load). Load the roof rack with the largest items at the rear, and the smallest items at the front (to help minimise wind resistance). Wrap the plastic or tarpaulin around the load, trying to arrange the overlap so that the wind won't catch it. Secure it with suitable tie-downs (use the self-locking type with a metal buckle), rope, or elastic cords – an 'octopus'-style load bungee is ideal. Make sure the rack and load are secure – give them a good pull in all directions before setting off, and if necessary add additional securing straps. Remember, the load must be secured against sliding sideways, backwards and forwards.

Once you set off on your journey, stop after the first few miles to check that nothing's moved or worked loose.

ABOVE Roof bars allow a whole range of load-carrying systems to be fitted to a car, including roof boxes and cycle carriers

Roof boxes

These come in various sizes and shapes to suit almost every car. Their aerodynamic profile helps to cut down wind resistance, and most can be locked for added security.

Special roof boxes are available for carrying sports equipment such as skis, and these have purpose-designed fixings inside to keep the equipment secure without the risk of damage. Some narrow boxes can be fitted on one side of the roof bars, to allow a cycle carrier or other equipment to be fitted next to them.

BELOW Roof boxes come in a huge range of shapes and sizes to suit all tastes and requirements

As with many other things in life, you generally get what you pay for when buying roof boxes, although there's no doubt that you'll pay more for 'designer-look' boxes. Various different fixing systems are used, and some designs are better than others. Some boxes have quick-release fittings to make them easier to remove and refit, and it's possible to open the lid of some from either side of the car, which can be a big advantage if you're travelling abroad because you can unload the box without having to step into the road.

Think carefully about your needs, and buy a big enough box to suit the loads that you're likely to carry. Make sure that the box will fit your car – for instance, if you have a hatchback check the length of the box and make sure that the rear overhang won't foul the tailgate when it's fully open. Check the recommended maximum load weight for the box, and make sure that you don't overload it (similarly, make sure that you don't exceed the maximum roof load weight for the car, taking into account the weight of the box itself).

Most larger car accessory shops stock a good range of roof boxes, as do some camping specialists. There are also a number of internet-based specialists offering very competitive deals, but obviously, unless you live near the supplier you can't view before you buy if you choose this route.

Cycle carriers

A wide range of specialist cycle carriers is available, and which system suits you best is very much down to personal choice – but if you opt for a cycle carrier that fits on the rear of the car, the roof space will still be available to carry other loads. Most roof bar manufacturers also market compatible cycle carriers.

If you use a rear-mounted carrier, bear in mind that cars following you must still be able to read your car's rear number plate and see all the rear lights. You'll probably have to buy an additional rear number plate, and you may even have to fit a set of lights (and an appropriate wiring kit).

BELOW Both rear and roof-mounted cycle carriers are available to suit most cars, and some can carry several cycles

LEFT Many an unusual load has been carried home from a DIY centre! Make sure that large or heavy items are secure, and positioned clear of the driver

BELOW If your car's boot is big enough, and you're not carrying any other luggage, you may not need a cycle carrier!

Carrying long loads

If you have to carry an unusually long load, the best place to put it is on roof bars or on a roof rack. Make sure the load is properly secured, and can't slide forwards or backwards.

If you can't put the load on the roof, fold down the rear seats (if possible) and slide the load in beside the front passenger seat – you may be able to fold or recline this seat to give more room. Make sure the load is secure and doesn't interfere with the driver's controls. If you can't fully close the boot lid or tailgate, make sure it's held securely with rope or a tie-down, and make sure that the number plate and rear lights are still visible.

Any load extending more than 0.3m beyond the car's rear bumper should have a prominent red flag attached to it.

Safety when carrying heavy loads

Before you start loading the car, consider the safety (and legal) implications.

- Load the car sensibly – how many cars have you seen driving back from the ferry port full of 'duty-free', with the rear bodywork touching the tyres and the headlights pointing at the sky? If the suspension can't do its job it's dangerous, and it's also likely to cause damage to the car. Make sure your headlight beams are adjusted to compensate for any load.
- Never exceed the 'maximum gross vehicle weight' – this will be given in your car's handbook.

- Make sure that the load doesn't affect your visibility – if you can't see through the back window, make sure that your door mirrors are adjusted so that you can still see behind you. Never allow anything to hang down over the windscreen.
- Increase your tyre pressures when carrying a heavy load – consult your car's handbook for details. You may need to inflate your tyres to the 'full-load' pressures.
- Make sure that your car's rear number plate and lights are visible – it's against the law to drive with a number plate or light obscured, and it's dangerous.

Towing

Towing a trailer or a caravan for the first time might seem a rather nerve-racking prospect, but provided you prepare properly and know what to expect – and, of course, you remember that you have a trailer behind you – it's really not that different to normal driving.

Preparing a car for towing

If you're towing for the first time, there are a few points to bear in mind. First, make sure your car's fitted with a tow bar which is up to the job! If you can afford it, it's worth paying for a professional installation.

Make sure your car can cope with the load – are the engine, brakes, tyres and suspension adequate for towing the trailer or caravan you have in mind?

Make sure that you know the weight of your trailer or caravan, and check the maximum recommended trailer or tow-bar weight for your car, which mustn't be exceeded.

Sit in the driver's seat and make sure you can see behind the trailer/caravan using your car's wing mirrors. If you can't, extending side mirrors or special temporary towing mirrors can be fitted to most cars.

Make sure the tyre pressures for your car and the trailer/caravan are correct. Unless you're towing a light, unladen trailer, the car tyres should be inflated to the 'full load' pressures – check your car's handbook for details.

Make sure that the car's headlights are set correctly – check the aim with the trailer/caravan attached, and adjust it if necessary. Many cars have an adjuster switch on the dashboard, and recommended positions for towing can usually be found in the car handbook.

Make sure that the trailer/caravan lights work correctly. The extra load on your car's flasher circuit may cause the indicators to flash too slowly, so you may need a 'heavy duty' flasher unit, available from most good car accessory shops and caravan specialists. Note that if you're travelling abroad, in some countries you need to have a separate warning light fitted in the car to show that the trailer/caravan direction indicator lights are working.

If you're planning on towing a particularly heavy load, the extra demand placed on the engine may mean that the cooling system is no longer adequate. You may be able to have modified cooling system components (a larger radiator, etc) fitted to cope with this if you tow regularly, but provided you have a reasonably powerful car this shouldn't be necessary.

Towing also puts extra strain on a car's suspension components, and can affect its handling. Heavy-duty rear suspension components are available for most cars, and if you're going to tow a heavy load such as a caravan regularly, it's sensible to have upgraded components fitted.

If you're going to tow a caravan or a large, high-sided trailer, consider buying a stabiliser. A stabiliser reduces the risk of 'snaking', which can be a problem if the trailer or caravan is loaded unevenly, or if you're driving in a sidewind.

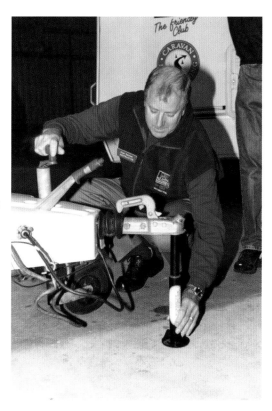

Driving tips for towing

Make sure that you're familiar with any laws that apply to towing, especially if you're travelling abroad. In particular, make sure that you know the relevant speed limits – in most countries, lower limits apply when towing.

Before setting off on a journey, make sure that the trailer/caravan is correctly loaded – refer to the manufacturer's recommendations for details. As a general rule, distribute the weight with the heaviest items as near as possible to the trailer/caravan axle, and secure all heavy items so that they can't move. Car manufacturers usually specify an optimum 'noseweight' for a trailer/caravan when loaded. The noseweight is the downward load that the trailer or caravan puts on the tow ball when connected. The noseweight can be checked with a special gauge available from car accessory shops, or by using bathroom scales and a suitable length of wood (so that the trailer coupling rests on the scales at the same height it will be at when connected to the car's tow ball) under the trailer coupling. If necessary, move the load in the trailer/caravan to get as close as possible to the recommended noseweight. Never exceed the recommended noseweight.

Avoid driving with an unladen car and a loaded trailer/caravan – the uneven weight distribution will make the car unstable.

LEFT Checking a caravan noseweight using a special gauge – car manufacturers usually specify an optimum noseweight

LEFT Temporary towing mirrors are often essential when towing a caravan or a wide trailer

Always drive at a safe speed. Reduce speed in bad weather and high winds, especially when driving downhill. If there are any signs of 'snaking', slow down immediately but gently – never try to solve the problem by accelerating or braking hard.

Always brake in good time. If the trailer/caravan has brakes, apply the brakes gently at first, then firmly. This will prevent the trailer/caravan wheels from locking. If the car has a manual transmission, change to a lower gear before driving down a steep hill (the engine will act as a brake), and on cars with automatic transmission, select '2', or '1' in the case of very steep hills.

Don't use a lower gear unnecessarily. Stay in as high a gear as possible, to keep the engine revs low, but don't let the engine struggle. This helps to avoid engine overheating.

Reversing when towing

Make sure that you know how to reverse – this can be tricky if you've never tried before. It's a great help to have an assistant, to look out for obstructions and other vehicles, and to give you reassurance.

When reversing with a trailer or caravan, you need to get used to the fact that you need to turn the car's steering wheel in the opposite direction to where you want the trailer or caravan to go. This can be a tricky concept to get used to, but with a little prastice it will become second nature.

As with many things, practice makes perfect, and it's a good idea to build up confidence by practising in an open space, such as a quiet car park, or perhaps an old airfield (with the owner's permission of course), before you venture out onto the road.

Reversing in a straight line

When reversing in a straight line, a helpful rule to follow is to steer towards the wing mirror in which the trailer or caravan appears.

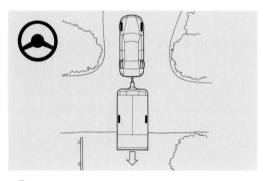

1 Start reversing exactly as you would normally – with the steering wheel in the straight-ahead position.

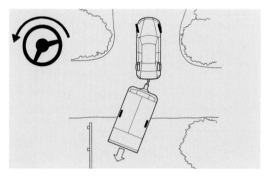

2 Check each side mirror in turn, and if you see the back end of the trailer or caravan appearing in one of them, steer smoothly towards that mirror to straighten up. So, if the trailer or caravan appears in the left mirror, move the steering wheel to the left.

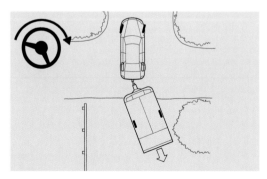

3 Check each mirror in turn, and if the trailer/caravan begins to veer, again steer towards the mirror in which it appears. Only make very slight movements.

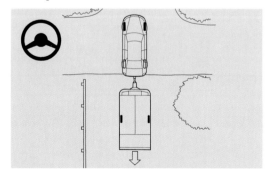

4 By keeping a careful eye on both mirrors, and making continual small corrections, you should soon be able to reverse in a straight line instinctively.

Reversing round corners

Once you've mastered reversing in a straight line, reversing round corners shouldn't prove too difficult, as you'll already have a feel for the technique required. If possible get an assistant to help, as if you're a standard-spec human you won't be able to see round corners! Don't try to reverse any faster than a slow walking pace, so that you can anticipate and correct any mistakes early on.

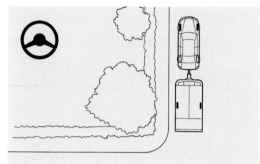

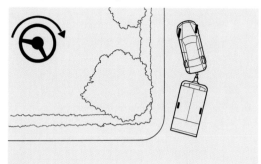

1 To reverse around a left-hand corner, keep the car and trailer/caravan aligned as you start to go back in a straight line, then turn the steering wheel to the right.

2 As you turn the steering wheel right, the trailer or caravan will start to move to the left. As it starts to turn the corner, keep looking ahead, and check the mirrors as the car starts to swing out, as you would normally. Be prepared to stop to allow other traffic to pass safely.

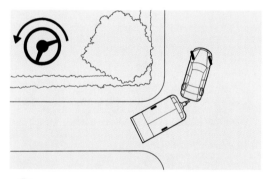

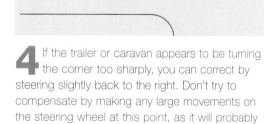

3 Once the trailer or caravan has started to turn the corner, change the direction of the steering wheel and turn it to the left, which will keep the trailer/caravan moving round the corner in a smooth arc.

4 If the trailer or caravan appears to be turning the corner too sharply, you can correct by steering slightly back to the right. Don't try to compensate by making any large movements on the steering wheel at this point, as it will probably make things worse.

5 If you don't manage to correct in time, and the trailer or caravan has already cornered too sharply, stop. If you carry on, the trailer or caravan may 'jack-knife' and the front of it may contact the back of the car, causing damage. If you think you may be about to jack-knife, stop and pull forwards a short distance until the car and trailer/caravan are straight, then try again.

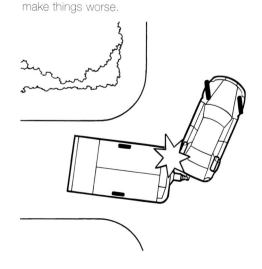

6 To reverse around a right-hand corner, simply follow the opposite procedure. In a right-hand-drive car you should find it slightly easier to reverse round a right-hand corner, as you'll be able to look out of your side window.

Preparing
for a holiday

If you're taking your car on holiday, you want to be able to relax, so before you set off it's worth planning ahead and making sure that your car has been serviced properly.

Planning ahead

It's a good idea to plan your route before travelling, and to make sure that you have a good road atlas or map in the car. Many different maps and guides are available, and most of the motoring organisations will provide a set of directions to your destination, often through their websites. When planning your route, bear in mind that you may have to pay tolls to use certain roads, particularly abroad, and you may choose to avoid these roads if the charges are high.

If you're travelling a long way allow time for any hold-ups, and either make sure that you take a break if you start to feel tired, or share the driving. On long journeys with children, make sure that they have enough to do to keep them amused.

When travelling abroad, make sure that you have all the documentation you need before you set off, and make sure that your car meets any regulations that are specific to the country you're visiting.

If your car is approaching one of its service intervals, it's worth thinking about having it serviced before you travel, to minimise the risk of trouble. Always check the tyre pressures, fluid levels, bulbs, wiper blades, etc, before setting off – refer to Chapter 5 for more details.

When loading up, take care not to overload your car, and make sure that any items you're likely to need during the journey (including your tool kit) are packed so that they're easily accessible.

Travelling abroad

There are a few extra considerations to bear in mind when driving abroad. For a comprehensive guide, with specific details for most common destination countries, refer to *Driving Abroad*, also published by Haynes Publishing.

Insurance

Check on the legal requirements for the country you're visiting, and always tell your insurance company that you're taking the car abroad. If you're travelling in the European Community (EC), most insurance policies automatically give only the minimum legally required cover. If you want the same level of cover as you have at home you'll usually have to pay a small extra premium.

It's a good idea to take out medical insurance. Not all countries have a free emergency medical service, and you could find yourself faced with a large unexpected bill. With a travel insurance policy, you're usually covered for any money lost if you have to cancel your holiday, and your luggage may also be covered against loss or theft. Make sure you take the time to read the small print so that you know exactly what's covered!

Recovery and breakdown costs can be far higher abroad. Most of the motoring organisations will be able to provide breakdown insurance cover for travel abroad, which could save you a lot of inconvenience and expense.

Driving laws

Make sure you're familiar with the driving laws in the country you're visiting – the penalties for breaking the law may be severe! You may be legally required to carry certain safety equipment

such as spare light bulbs, a warning triangle, and a first aid kit.

If you're driving on the opposite side of the road from normal, you'll need to fit headlight beam deflectors to avoid dazzling other drivers.

Make sure that you know the appropriate speed limits, and note that in some countries there's an absolute ban on driving after drinking any alcohol.

Fuel

The type and quality of fuel available varies from country to country. Check on availability, and find out what fuel pump markings to look for to ensure that you can find the correct type and grade of fuel for your car. You don't want to have to try and explain to the pump attendant that you've just put diesel in your petrol car!

Documents

Always carry your passport, driving licence, vehicle registration document, vehicle test certificate, and insurance certificate(s) (including medical and breakdown insurance where applicable) – but don't leave them in the car unattended!

Make sure that all the documents are valid, and that the road tax and MoT certificate don't run out while you're abroad.

Before travelling, check in case any special documents or permits are required. You may need a visa to visit some countries, and an international driving permit (available from the major motoring organisations) may be required.

BELOW When travelling abroad, always check what documents you're required by law to carry in the country you're visiting

Economical
driving

Economical driving isn't everyone's first priority, but it's surprising how driving style can affect fuel consumption, and how relatively easy it can be to save on fuel costs.

Fuel

For the majority of people, by far the biggest expense involved in running a car is the cost of fuel. If you've got into the habit of filling your car with fuel regularly, have you stopped to work out how much it's costing you over a year? This is worth thinking about when you're considering replacing your car.

Depending on where you live, 'own-brand' supermarket fuel may be significantly cheaper than branded fuel from a garage or service station. It may also be more convenient for you to fill up when you do your shopping. The oil companies will argue that their own branded fuels contain beneficial additives that aren't necessarily included in supermarket fuel. There's no definite answer to the question of whether the branded fuels are worth the extra cost, but it's true to say that supermarket fuel meets the appropriate national standards and you certainly won't cause any serious damage to your car by using it.

Driving style

The biggest influence on fuel consumption is driving style. Basically, the smoother the driving style, the more economical it will be. You'll also find that fuel consumption increases rapidly when the cruising speed goes up. The following factors all increase fuel consumption.

- Taking the engine to high revs before changing gear.
- Heavy braking.
- Hard acceleration.
- Sitting in traffic jams.
- Towing, or carrying a heavy load.
- Fitting roof bars or a roof box (which increases wind resistance, even when empty).
- Frequent short journeys (more fuel's used when the engine is cold).
- Long journeys in strong headwinds.
- Long distances driving up or down steep hills.
- Abnormally hot or cold weather.

Money saving tips

- Drive smoothly – your fuel bills will be lower, and you'll also avoid wear and tear.
- Try to avoid traffic jams – if stuck, switch off your engine.
- Check tyre pressures regularly – under-inflated tyres increase fuel consumption.
- Avoid short journeys – the engine will use more fuel when it's cold.
- Consider buying supermarket fuel if it's significantly cheaper.
- Think about doing at least some of your own maintenance to save on servicing costs.

BELOW Sitting in a traffic jam with the engine running is one of the worst scenarios for fuel consumption

Driving in
bad weather

When driving in bad weather, always be prepared. Driving in bad weather requires more concentration, and is more tiring than driving in good weather. Always look well ahead so that you're aware of the condition of the road surface and any obstacles, and slow down if necessary.

The following hints and tips will help you to avoid trouble in bad weather, but there's no substitute for common sense.

Rain
When driving in heavy rain:

- Use dipped headlights in poor visibility.
- Slow down if visibility is poor, or if there's a lot of water on the road surface.
- Keep a safe distance from any vehicles in front – stopping distances can be doubled on a wet road surface.
- Be especially careful when it rains after a long period of dry weather. In these conditions rain

will wash grease, spilt diesel fuel and other deposits out of the road surface, making it very slippery.

■ Don't use rear fog lights unless visibility is seriously reduced – fog lights can dazzle drivers following behind, especially in motorway spray.

Fog

When driving in foggy conditions:

■ Slow down – fog is deceptive, and you may be driving faster than you think. Fog can also be patchy, and the visibility may be suddenly reduced. Try to drive at a speed that will allow you to stop in the distance you can see ahead.

■ Use dipped headlights, and in thick fog switch on front fog lights if you have them, which will help to illuminate the road surface. Using main beam headlights will usually reduce the visibility even further, as the fog will scatter the light.

■ Use rear fog lights in thick fog to give following drivers a better chance of seeing you.

■ Keep a safe distance from the vehicle in front.

■ Use your windscreen wipers to clear moisture from the windscreen.

Frost, ice and snow

In very cold weather, when there's a risk of freezing, or if there's frost, ice or snow on the road:

■ Check the weather forecast before you set off, and don't start a journey if there's a possibility that the conditions may prevent you from reaching your destination.

■ Before starting a journey, clear all ice or snow from the windscreen, windows and mirrors. Don't just clear a small area big enough to see through, as it may take a long time for the rest of the glass to clear once you start driving – it may not clear at all if it's very cold.

■ Keep a safe distance from any vehicle in front – stopping distances can increase by up to four times on a snow-covered or icy surface.

■ Use main roads and motorways where possible. Major roads are likely to have been gritted and are usually cleared before minor roads.

■ Refer to the next section for more advice on driving in wintry conditions.

ABOVE It's important to make sure that your windscreen wipers are in good condition, so that you can see clearly when driving in rain

BELOW Fog can be extremely hazardous when driving – slow down, and use dipped headlights and foglights

Winter driving

Winter puts extra strain on a car's systems, and any minor problems that have been lurking under the surface are likely to become more obvious and may cause trouble once winter gets a grip.

Getting ready for winter

In cold conditions it takes more power to start the engine, you'll be using the heater and demister more often and the heated rear window and heated windscreen if your car has one, and of course since there's less light in the winter months you'll be using the headlights more as well – this all takes its toll on the battery.

It's a good idea to check your car thoroughly before winter arrives, to minimise the risk of trouble. Here's a pre-winter checklist, which should help you to avoid the more common winter problems. Details of how to make the checks are given in Chapter 5.

Pre-winter checklist

- Check the condition of the battery, and fit a new one if necessary.
- Check the condition of the coolant, and make sure that there's enough antifreeze in the coolant mixture.
- Check the condition of the wiper blades, and fit new ones if necessary.
- Check that the washer nozzles are not blocked.
- Check the auxiliary drivebelt(s).
- Check all the fluid levels.
- Check the lights and indicators.

Driving in wintry conditions

The onset of winter shouldn't pose any problems, as long as you're suitably equipped. Even during a mild winter you're likely to encounter some frosty mornings, so before winter arrives it's a good idea to add an ice scraper and a can of de-icer to your tool kit.

If you're not already a member, it's worthwhile considering joining one of the motoring breakdown organisations – it will provide you with peace of mind, and could save you a lot of trouble and expense if the worst happens.

When driving on slippery roads, drive slowly, smoothly and gently – accelerate gently, steer gently and brake gently, and keep the engine revs as low as possible. Always try to stay in the highest gear possible, and if the road is very slippery try moving off from rest using second gear instead of first – this will help to avoid wheelspin. If the wheels do start to spin, don't accelerate harder, as this will just make things worse – do exactly the opposite and back off on the accelerator, which should help the wheels to regain grip.

Severe winter weather

If severe winter weather is expected (prolonged snow or heavy freezing), the best advice is to stay at home unless a journey is absolutely essential. The weather can worsen very quickly in winter, so even if it looks OK when you set off, be prepared! If you can't avoid driving in severe cold, or snowy and icy conditions, make sure you're properly equipped. If you're planning a journey of any distance it's a good idea to carry a set of jump leads and a tow-rope, which will help to get you out of trouble in most situations. Carry warm clothes and blankets to keep you warm if you get stuck. A bar of chocolate could also come in handy!

Tell someone where you're going, what route you're taking, and what time you're expecting to arrive at your destination. Make sure that you have a full tank of fuel – this will allow you to keep the engine running for warmth (through the heating system) if you get delayed or stuck, without fear of running out of fuel. If you have a mobile phone make sure the battery's charged and if you have a 'pay-as-you-go' mobile, make sure your credit is topped up.

It's a good idea to pack some pieces of old sacking, or similar material, which you can place under the wheels to give better traction if you get stuck. You could also pack a shovel in case you need to dig yourself out of trouble.

Although it probably isn't worth buying them for use in the UK, in some countries it's compulsory to use snow chains or studded tyres on certain roads (or even all roads!) – note, however, that it may also be compulsory to remove them again when you reach roads which are unaffected by ice or snow (this applies to many alpine roads at certain times of the year).

LEFT Driving in snow for the first time can be daunting, but drive slowly and smoothly and you should stay out of trouble

Driving
with children

The most important consideration when travelling with children in a car is to make sure that they're safe. It can be difficult to keep children amused on a long journey, which can make it a stressful experience for the driver and any other passengers. Hopefully, the following advice will be helpful in keeping everyone happy!

Choosing a car seat

Most parents strap their children into child car seats, confident that they've done everything possible to protect their loved-ones. However, many young children are travelling in car seats that have been badly fitted, or are being incorrectly used, making them potentially dangerous if the worst happens and they're involved in an accident.

Never allow children to travel in a car unrestrained, even for the shortest of journeys, and never carry a child on an adult's lap or in an adult's arms – you may feel that your baby is safer in your arms, but this isn't the case. A purpose-designed car seat is the only safe way to carry a young child in a car.

Think very hard before buying a second-hand child seat, unless you know it's history and you're sure that all the parts are there and that the instructions come with it.

The weight, size and age of a child will determine the best type of child seat to use. All new seats will have a recommended suitable age and weight range, but these are only a rough guide. It's the weight of the child that's important – for instance, a smaller-than-average baby can use a baby seat for longer than a heavy baby of the same age.

There are a huge number of child seats on the market, and at first the choice can be baffling. It's worth noting that all new child seats must conform to United Nations Regulation No.44 (ECE R44.03). Child seats are available in a wide variety of designs and with various different fitting methods, but seats can be broadly divided in to the following groups:

Rearward-facing baby seats

- Can be used in the front or rear of the car.
- Allow the driver or passenger to see the baby more easily.
- Provide greater protection for the baby's head, neck and spine than a forward-facing seat.
- Have a built-in harness.
- Must not be used in the front passenger seat of a car with a passenger's airbag – unless the airbag can be deactivated.
- Group 0 – suitable for babies up to 10kg (22lb), or from birth to approx 6–9 months.
- Group 0+ – suitable for babies up to 13kg (29lb), or from birth to approx 12–15 months.

Forward-facing child seats

- Can be used in the front or rear of the car, but safer in the rear, especially if a passenger's airbag is fitted.
- Have a built-in harness.
- Group 1 – suitable for children from approx 9–18kg (20–40lb), or approx 9 months to 4 years.

Booster seat

- Can be used in the front or rear of the car, but safer in the rear, especially if a passenger's airbag is fitted.
- No built-in harness – relies on the car's seat belt to restrain the child. (Some types may have a built-in harness that can be removed when the child outgrows it.)
- Some types can be converted into a booster cushion by removing the backrest.
- Group 2 – suitable for children from approx 15–25kg (33–55lb), or approx 4–6 years.

Booster cushion

- Can be used in the front or rear of the car, but safer in the rear, especially if a passenger's airbag is fitted.
- No built-in harness – relies on a car's seat belt to restrain the child.
- Group 3 – suitable for children from approx 22–36kg (48–79lb), or approx 6–11 years.

Choose a seat which has an easily adjustable harness – this will ensure that the harness fits the child securely for each trip, and also makes life easier if your little passenger isn't in a cooperative mood!

Always follow the manufacturer's fitting instructions. As a general rule, the harness should be worn as tightly as possible, without hurting the child, lap belts should rest across the pelvis not the stomach, and shoulder straps should rest on the shoulders not the neck.

If your car is involved in any kind of serious impact, renew the child seat.

BELOW A rearward-facing child seat allows the driver to see the baby more clearly and provides improved head and neck protection

RIGHT Boredom is probably the biggest problem when travelling on a long journey with children!

Carsickness

Carsickness is just one of those things that some parents have to cope with – some children never suffer from carsickness, but some suffer frequently. All you can do as a driver is try to drive smoothly and provide a comfortable ride. Make sure that it isn't too stuffy inside the car (turn the heater down if necessary), and if possible leave a window (or the sunroof) open to allow fresh air in.

There are a number of forms of medication available to combat carsickness, but you should always read the instructions – if you're planning to give medication to a young child, it's vital to check that it's suitable. Don't exceed the recommended dosage.

If carsickness is likely to be a problem, carry a supply of sickbags and disinfectant wipes, and keep a bottle of clean water and some cloths on board for emergency cleaning operations. It's also a good plan to carry an air freshener!

Keeping a child amused

Young children need to be kept amused when travelling in a car, so make sure that they have a toy or two that they can play with without distracting the driver.

Every child's different, and children are amused in different ways depending on their age and temperament. If children could be persuaded to sleep or read during a journey, life would be a lot easier for the driver! Babies might well sleep most of the time in the car, but unless you're very lucky this probably won't be the case as they get older. As children grow up, reading is a great idea, but not all children are going to want to read every time they go on a long journey, and sometimes reading can actually provoke carsickness.

It's a case of seeing what works best for each individual child, but it's worth encouraging games that involve concentrating on what's going on outside the car, such as 'I-Spy', or car and truck spotting.

There are plenty of children's music and story tapes and CDs available, and a favourite story or song can work wonders. If you're planning to make a long journey or you're taking a motoring holiday, it might be worth buying a portable DVD player if your budget will allow it. These have become relatively inexpensive – some types are designed specifically for use in cars, and can be operated from the car's electrical system. Models are even available with two screens that can be attached to the rear of the front seat headrests, thereby avoiding squabbles over the best view of the screen. Most also have headphones to avoid distractions for the driver.

You could always try a spot of communal singing – depending on the musical tastes and abilities of the passengers of course!

BELOW In-car and portable DVD players are now commonplace, and are available as a built-in option on some models

Advanced driving

Once you've been driving for a while, you may be interested in taking an advanced driving course, which can help to improve your driving and can make a significant difference to your car insurance premium. Most courses give you the option to take a test at the end, which will provide you with a certificate to prove that you've successfully completed the course.

Various organisations offer advanced driving courses, including the RAC, the RoSPA, and the Institute of Advanced Motorists (IAM). The IAM course is perhaps the best known.

Most advanced driving instructors are serving or retired police drivers, so you can be sure that you'll be receiving the very best instruction.

Advanced courses concentrate on the following areas:

■ Increasing the driver's awareness of what's happening outside the car, which helps them to assess risks and avoid trouble.

■ Improving the smoothness with which the driver uses the car's controls, which improves control and reduces wear and tear on the car.

■ Improving driving skill and confidence.

Advanced driving courses are extremely worthwhile, and in most cases the cost of the course will be covered by the savings you'll make on you car insurance, if you obtain a certificate to prove that you've passed the course.

A list of organisations providing advanced driving courses can be found in Appendix C.

Track days
and race schools

Track days are growing in popularity, and offer a chance to explore your driving ability – and your car's capabilities – at high speed in the safe environment of a racetrack.

Most organisations running track days will offer the option of having instruction before you venture out on to the track on your own, and this is highly recommended. Be under no illusion that driving on a track is a very different proposition to driving on the road, and should not be underestimated. Speeds are much higher, driving has to be very smooth, and you'll have to learn to judge 'racing lines' and braking distances. It goes without saying that the stress on a car is far higher on the track than on the road, and the engine, brakes, tyres and suspension must be up to the job. Track day organisers will be able to advise you on how to avoid overstressing your car, and if the bug bites you, you may decide to modify your car for regular track day use, or even to invest in a purpose-built track-day car. Race schools offer the chance to drive a purpose-built racing car on the track, and the techniques learnt will benefit your road driving even if you never intend to compete in a race. A day at a racing or rally school will also help you to appreciate just how skilful professional competition drivers are!

Emergencies

The following pages contain some useful advice on what to do in various emergency situations. Much of it is common sense, but it's worth reading through it at leisure so that you're better prepared if you're unfortunate enough to face any of the situations mentioned.

Breakdowns

If you're unfortunate enough to break down on the road, try to keep calm, and think logically. You may not know what's wrong, but don't panic – the majority of breakdowns are caused by simple problems which can easily be fixed at the roadside by a good mechanic.

Much of the following advice is given with women driving alone particularly in mind, but it applies equally to any driver.

Breakdown assistance

There's really no substitute for belonging to one of the motoring breakdown organisations. Think of your membership as an insurance policy that will provide peace of mind if your car lets you down. There's a wide range of membership options to suit most requirements, and it's reassuring to know that help is only a phone call away.

If you do break down, being a member of a rescue service is actually likely to save you money. If you break down and you don't belong to one of the motoring organisations, you'll have to arrange for roadside assistance or recovery to a garage – this will almost certainly cost you more than a year's membership fee. Even if you only choose the basic minimum membership package from one of the smaller organisations, you'll easily save more than your membership fee the first time you have to call on their services. Some membership packages will give you the option of being transported to your intended destination or back home and, for an additional fee, will also provide breakdown cover if you take your car abroad. You may also have the temporary use of a hire car if your car can't be repaired quickly. Don't forget that most of the motoring organisations will also recover members' cars from the scene of an accident.

Breakdowns on ordinary roads

Try to stop where there are other people about. If possible, move the car out of the way of other traffic, then switch on the hazard warning lights and set up your warning triangle if you have one. Lift the bonnet – this will indicate to other motorists and any passing police patrol vehicles that you have a problem.

If your car is in a dangerous position, move yourself and any passengers away from the car to a safe place clear of the passing traffic.

If you have a mobile phone, call for assistance – if not, and you need to walk to find help, always take any young children with you. When asking for help, give details of:

1 Your motoring organisation membership number (if applicable).
2 Whether you're alone, or with young children.
3 Your location.
4 Your car make, colour and registration number.
5 The likely cause of the breakdown, or any symptoms.

Don't worry if you don't have all this information.

Once help is on its way, return to your car and, unless there's a danger of other traffic hitting it, stay inside the car, lock the doors, close the windows, and wait for help. If your car is in a dangerous position, move yourself and any passengers to a safe place where you can watch for help arriving.

If you're in your car and someone stops to offer help, talk to him or her through a closed window until you're absolutely sure that you can trust him or her. Always ask for identification. It must be a personal decision to accept help – or not.

LEFT Using a warning triangle if you suffer a breakdown will help to warn other motorists, improving safety

Breakdowns on a motorway

At the first sign of trouble, switch on the car's hazard warning lights, then pull onto the hard shoulder and park as far away as possible from the main carriageway. Get out of the car using the passenger's side door (taking any children with you), and if you have a mobile phone use it to contact your motoring organisation or the police.

If you don't have a mobile phone, walk to the nearest emergency telephone, keeping well to the inside of the hard shoulder. Arrows on marker posts at the edge of the hard shoulder indicate the direction to the nearest emergency phone – the phones will link you to a control centre. When you use the phone, face oncoming traffic. Tell the operator on the other end of the phone:

1 Your exact location – all motorway junctions are numbered, and so are the emergency phones.
2 Whether you're alone, or with young children.
3 Your motoring organisation membership number (if applicable).
4 Your car make, colour and registration number.
5 The likely cause of the breakdown, or any symptoms.

Don't worry if you don't have all this information.

Return to your car, but stand well away, behind the safety barrier and up the embankment if possible, and don't get back into your car unless you feel at risk – fatal accidents occur on the hard shoulder.

The most common causes of call-outs reported by the motoring organisations vary slightly each year, but averaged out over the last few years, the top ten causes of breakdowns are as follows:

1 Flat or faulty battery

To help to avoid problems:

- Check the battery terminals regularly, make sure that they're secure and keep them free from corrosion. Most car accessory shops sell battery terminal protector spray, or you can use petroleum jelly or grease instead.
- Keep the top of the battery clean and dry.
- If you make lots of short journeys, take your car on a long journey every once in a while, which will help the alternator to charge the battery.
- Make sure that all the electrical equipment (lights, heater blower, heated rear window, etc) is turned off before you try to start the engine.
- Check the alternator drivebelt once in a while.
- At the first sign of trouble, such as difficult starting, dim headlights, or if the charging warning light comes on, have the battery tested.

2 Flat or damaged tyres or wheels

To help to avoid problems:

- Check the tyre pressures and the condition of the tyres regularly. Don't forget the spare.
- Make sure that if you're carrying a heavy load you adjust the tyre pressures to the recommended 'full-load' pressures, and that you return them to normal when you've unloaded.
- If you 'kerb' a wheel when parking or driving, check the condition of the wheel and tyre as soon as possible afterwards.
- Consider carrying a can of tyre 'instant repair' foam.
- Make sure that the jack, wheel brace and (where applicable) the key or removal tool for locking wheel bolts, are in the car and that you know how to use them.

3 Alternator faults

The alternator's job is to charge the battery, and if the alternator fails, the battery will soon fail too. The telltale signs of a problem include:

- Frequent battery problems and dim headlights when the engine is ticking over.
- A squealing sound from the engine compartment, which may indicate a slipping alternator drivebelt.
- A glowing charging warning light (usually orange), especially when the engine is ticking over.
- Stop as soon as possible if the charging warning light comes on when you're driving.

4 Starter motor failure

The following signs are likely to indicate that the starter motor has failed:

- Metallic noises when trying to start the engine.
- The engine turns more slowly than usual when you try to start it (might also indicate a battery problem).
- A click can be heard from the engine compartment, but the engine doesn't turn over when the key is turned to the 'start' position (might also indicate a battery problem).

5 Ignition distributor cap or rotor arm problems

Many modern cars don't have a distributor cap, so this may not apply to your car. It doesn't apply to cars with diesel engines. To help to avoid trouble, make sure that the distributor cap and rotor arm are checked when your car is serviced. The telltale signs of a problem include:

- Misfiring of the engine, especially when accelerating or driving uphill.
- Difficulty starting the engine, especially in damp weather.

6 Running out of fuel or filling with the wrong type of fuel

Both of these problems are easily avoidable, provided you take the following precautions:

- Fill up with fuel before a long journey.
- Keep an eye on your fuel gauge, and don't wait until the warning light comes on before filling up. Fuel gauges can be notoriously inaccurate!
- If you're travelling on a road where fuel stations are scarce, make sure you have enough fuel to make it to the next large town where there's likely to be fuel available.
- If you're driving a new car, or you've hired or borrowed a car, make sure you know what type of fuel it takes, and always make sure that you've selected the correct fuel pump (petrol or diesel) before starting to fill up.

7 Damage to clutch cables

This only applies to cars with a manual gearbox, and even then some cars have a hydraulic clutch which doesn't use a cable. If the clutch cable breaks, you won't be able to change gear – nothing will happen when you press the clutch pedal. To help to avoid trouble, make sure that the clutch cable is checked when your car is serviced. Telltale signs of a problem include:

- The clutch feels 'strange' when you press the clutch pedal, or the pedal seems to be higher or lower than normal when in its rest position.
- The gears crunch when changing gear.

8 Neglected spark plugs

This only applies to cars with a petrol engine. To help to avoid problems, new spark plugs should be fitted at the intervals recommended by the car manufacturer. The telltale signs of a problem include:

- Misfiring of the engine, especially when accelerating or driving uphill.
- Difficulty starting the engine, especially in damp weather.

9 Faults with ignition HT leads

This only applies to cars with a petrol engine. The HT leads connect the spark plugs to the coil, and they deteriorate with age. To help to avoid problems, keep the HT leads clean and make sure that they're connected securely. The telltale signs of a problem include:

- Misfiring of the engine, especially when accelerating or driving uphill.
- Difficulty starting the engine, especially in damp weather.

10 Leaking cylinder head gasket

A leaking cylinder head gasket can be a big problem, and major work on the engine may be required to fix it. There's little that can be done to avoid this problem, but a major cause is engine overheating, so keep an eye on the temperature gauge from time to time, and if the temperature creeps towards the red zone stop immediately and check the coolant level. The telltale signs of a problem include:

- A lack of power.
- Misfiring, especially when the engine is cold or when starting.
- Fluid leaks on the outside of the engine.
- Oil in the coolant – usually shows itself as a frothy 'mayonnaise'.
- Coolant in the oil – usually shows itself as a frothy 'mayonnaise'.
- A mysterious drop in coolant level and the need for frequent topping up.

LEFT A flat tyre will halt your journey, but changing a wheel is straightforward provided your spare wheel/tyre and tools are in good condition

Stiff wheel bolts

Sometimes it's difficult to loosen the wheel bolts or nuts, and if you have a new tyre fitted some fitters have a habit of using an air-wrench overenthusiastically to tighten the bolts, making it very difficult to loosen them for the first time afterwards.

If you've recently had new tyres fitted, it's a good idea to loosen the wheel bolts when you get home, and tighten them again yourself using the car's wheel brace, making sure of course that you tighten them enough.

To make things easier you can buy a wheel brace with an extending handle from most good motoring accessory shops, or alternatively you can carry a length of metal tube to fit over the wheel brace for more leverage.

'Space-saver' spare tyres

Some cars have a space-saver spare wheel and tyre because there isn't enough room in the car for a normal full-size spare.

These tyres are narrower than normal tyres, and are often inflated to a different pressure. There are usually speed and mileage restrictions marked on the tyre, or printed in the car handbook – make sure you take note of these restrictions.

If you fit a space-saver tyre, have the 'normal' flat tyre repaired and refitted as soon as possible.

How to change a wheel

Changing a wheel is straightforward provided you know where the tools and spare wheel are kept, and how to use the jack. If you've just bought the car, or if you've never changed a wheel before, it's worth practising at home, then you'll know exactly what to do if you get a flat tyre.

If you pick up a puncture when you're driving, you'll probably notice the car 'pulling' through the steering and, depending on how flat the tyre is, the car's handling is likely to be affected – the car may feel as if it's sliding, as on an icy road, when you turn a corner.

If you think your car may have a puncture, stop as soon as possible, but don't panic – heavy braking with a serious puncture could cause you to lose control. Try to park safely, away from traffic. If you're at the side of a busy road, and you can't move the car, it's safer to call for assistance rather than risk an accident. Stop the car, switch on the hazard warning lights, and set up your warning triangle, if you have one, to alert other road users, particularly in the dark.

Changing a wheel

1 Check that the car's parked on level ground, and make sure that the handbrake is applied. Select first gear (manual transmission) or 'P' (automatic transmission).

2 Get out the spare wheel, car jack and wheel brace. Chock the wheel diagonally opposite the one to be changed, using a couple of wooden blocks, or large stones.

3 Where applicable, pull off the wheel trim, then use the wheelbrace to loosen each wheel bolt/nut on the affected wheel by about half a turn.

4 Engage the jack head in the jacking point nearest the affected wheel (check your car's handbook for details). Slide the spare wheel part way under the side of the car, near the wheel to be removed, but out of the way of the jack (this is a safety measure). Raise the jack until the wheel is a few centimetres off the ground.

5 Remove the wheel bolts/nuts, and lift off the wheel. Drag the spare wheel out from under the side of the car, and slide the removed wheel under the car in its place.

6 Fit the spare wheel, then refit the bolts/nuts, and tighten them until they're just holding the wheel firmly.

7 Remove the wheel from under the car, then lower the jack and remove it from under the car.

8 Tighten one wheel bolt/nut securely, using the wheelbrace, then tighten the one diagonally opposite. Tighten the other two bolts/nuts in the same way, then refit the wheel trim where applicable.

9 When you've finished, stow the removed wheel and the tools back in their correct locations. Check the pressure in the 'new' tyre with your gauge or at the next available garage. It's important to get the flat tyre repaired or renewed as soon as possible, so that you have a spare if you're unlucky enough to get a second puncture.

Warning lights and what they mean

All cars are fitted with various warning lights to alert the driver to possible faults in its systems. Some warnings are more serious than others, so here's a guide to what the more common warning lights mean, and what to do if they come on. All the warning lights are usually explained in the car's handbook.

Warning light and what it means

What should I do?

Brake fluid level warning
■ Low brake fluid level.

■ Don't drive the car.
■ Check the brake fluid level and top up if necessary.
■ If the fluid level is low, have the car checked for brake fluid leaks, and don't drive it until the problem has been fixed.

Brake pad wear warning
■ Brake pads worn.

■ The car can be driven.
■ Have the pads checked and if necessary renewed as soon as possible.

Handbrake 'on' warning
■ Handbrake is applied.

■ Check the handbrake is released if you're about to drive off.

Charge warning
■ Alternator is not charging battery.

■ The car can be driven, but not too far, as the battery may eventually go flat.
■ Have the alternator and its wiring checked as soon as possible.

Oil pressure warning
■ Engine oil pressure low.

■ If the light comes on when the engine's ticking over, the engine may be very hot or worn. Check that the light goes out when you 'blip' the throttle.
■ Check the oil level as soon as possible.
■ If the light comes on when driving, stop the engine immediately, check the oil level and look for leaks, then call for assistance. Serious and expensive damage could be caused if you carry on running the engine.

Coolant temperature
■ Coolant temperature warning high.

■ Stop as soon as possible, allow the engine to cool, then check the coolant level. Top up if necessary.
■ If the light comes on again within a short distance, stop and call for assistance.

Coolant level warning
■ Coolant level low.

■ Stop as soon as possible, allow the engine to cool, then check the coolant level. Top up if necessary.
■ If the light comes on again within a short distance, check for leaks.

Engine system warning
■ Fault present.

■ The car can be driven, but you may notice a drop in performance. Have the engine management system checked as soon as possible.

ABS warning
■ ABS fault.

■ The car can be driven, but the ABS may not be working (normal braking won't be affected). Have the ABS tested as soon as possible.

Airbag (or SRS) warning
■ Airbag system fault.

■ The car can be driven, but the airbag system may not work. Have the airbag system checked as soon as possible.

Glow plug warning (diesel)
■ Glow plugs operating.

■ This is normal – wait for the light to go out before starting the engine.

Low fuel warning
■ Low fuel level in tank.

■ Fill up soon!

Accidents

If you're involved in an accident, or you find yourself on the scene of an accident, the first priority must be safety. This might seem obvious, but it's easy to overlook certain points which could make the situation worse – always try to think clearly, and don't panic!

What to do at the scene of an accident

1 Further collisions and fire are the main dangers in a road accident. To minimise the risk:

■ If possible, warn other traffic.
■ Switch on the car's hazard warning flashers.
■ Set up a warning triangle a reasonable distance away from the accident to warn approaching drivers. Decide from which direction the approaching traffic will have least warning, and position the triangle accordingly.
■ Send someone to warn approaching traffic of the danger, and signal the traffic to slow down.
■ Switch off the ignition and make sure no one smokes. This will reduce the possibility of a fire if there's a petrol leak.

2 If necessary, administer first aid if you've been properly trained.

3 Call the emergency services if necessary, bearing in mind the following:

■ Make sure that all the necessary information is given to the operator – give the exact location of the accident, the number of vehicles and, if applicable, the number of casualties involved.
■ Always ask for the police – they will decide whether they need to attend. In most cases, the accident must be reported to the police in any case within 24 hours.
■ Ask for an ambulance if anyone's seriously injured or trapped.
■ Ask for the fire brigade if anyone's trapped or if you think there's a risk of fire.

4 If you're involved in the accident, provide your personal and car details to anyone having reasonable grounds to ask for them. You should provide:

■ Your name and address.
■ Your car's registration number.
■ Details of your insurance company.

5 Essential details to record if you're involved in an accident.

The following details will help you fill in an accident report form for your insurance company, and will help if the police become involved. Inform your insurance company if you're involved in an accident, even if you're not going to make a claim. Make a note of:

■ The name and address of any other driver(s) involved, and those of the vehicle owner(s), if different.
■ The name(s) and address(es) of any witness(es). Independent witnesses are especially important.
■ A description of any injury to yourself or anyone else.
■ Details of any damage.
■ The insurance company details of any other driver(s) involved.
■ The registration number(s) of the other vehicle(s).
■ The number of any police officer attending the scene.
■ The location, time and date of the accident.
■ The speed of the vehicles involved.
■ The width of the road, details of road signs, the state of the road, and the weather.
■ Any relevant marks or debris on the road.
■ A rough sketch of the accident.
■ Whether the vehicle occupants were wearing seat belts.
■ If it happened at night or in bad weather, whether vehicle lights or streetlights were on.
■ If you have a camera, take pictures.
■ If the other driver refuses to give you his/her name and address, or if you think that he/she might have committed a criminal offence, inform the police immediately.

ABOVE The emergency services are experienced in dealing with the results of an accident – unless you've been properly trained, leave it to the professionals

What the law says you must do if you have an accident

If you're involved in an accident that causes damage or injury to any other person, another vehicle, an animal, or roadside property, you must:

- Stop.
- Give your own and the car owner's name and address, the registration number of the car, and your insurance details to anyone having reasonable grounds for requiring them.
- If you don't give your name and address to any such person at the time, report the accident to the police as soon as possible, and in any case within 24 hours.

Car theft

If you're unfortunate enough to have had your car stolen, here's a guide to what to do.

If you left the car in a car park, are you sure that you've returned to where you left it? This might sound obvious, but large car parks, especially multi-storeys, can be confusing!

The first thing to do if your car has been stolen is to contact the police, giving them the following information:

- Your name and address.
- The make, colour and registration number of your car.
- The last-known location of your car.
- The time that you left your car, and the time that you returned.
- Details of any important or valuable items left in the car.

After informing the police, contact your insurance company and give them the details that you provided to the police – you'll have to fill in a claim form later, but you should inform your insurance company by phone as soon as possible after the incident. Most insurance companies provide a helpline – they'll often arrange for you to be transported home, as will most of the motoring assistance organisations if you're a member.

Car break-ins and vandalism

If your car has been broken into or vandalised, first check to see if anything has been stolen, and write down the details of any stolen items. Next, check your car for damage – is there any damage that will stop you from driving the car (wiring, ignition switch, steering, etc), which may not be obvious at first?

Once you've checked your car, contact the police, and give them the following information:

- Your name and address.
- The make, colour and registration number of your car.
- The location of your car.
- The time that you left your car, and the time that you returned.
- Details of any damage, and details of any items stolen.

After informing the police, contact your insurance company – refer to the advice at the end of the previous section on Car theft for details.

BELOW Car crime is a serious problem, but taking sensible precautions to protect your car and it's contents will deter criminals

Towing a car

As a driver, towing a car – either driving the tow-car or the car being towed – can be quite tricky if you haven't tried it before. If you're not confident that you can tow successfully, or if you don't have the proper equipment or a car that's powerful enough to tow another car, the best advice is don't. It's far safer to call a recovery vehicle than to risk causing an accident. The following advice should provide you with all the information you need if you decide to tow.

Special towing eyes are normally provided at the front and rear of the car. Sometimes the towing eyes may be hidden under covers, and some cars have screw-in towing eyes provided in the tool kit – check your car's handbook for details.

You'll need a suitable tow-rope, and it needs to be of a sensible length – not too short or too long. It's worth carrying one just in case you ever need it.

If you've never towed before, take note of the following points.

■ When being towed, the ignition key must be turned to the 'on' position so that the steering lock is released. This will also allow the indicators, horn and brake lights to work. If the battery's flat or there's some other electrical problem, you'll have to use hand signals.

ABOVE Make sure that any slack in the tow-rope is taken up before moving off

LEFT Make sure that the tow-rope is securely attached to the tow car and the car being towed – check the instructions provided with the tow-rope for details

■ If you're driving a car that's being towed the brake servo won't work (because the engine isn't running). This means that you'll have to press the brake pedal harder than usual, so allow for longer braking distances. Also, power steering (where applicable) won't work when the engine isn't running, so you'll need more effort to turn the steering wheel. If the breakdown doesn't stop the engine running, you could allow it to idle so that the brake servo and power steering work normally, but make sure that you keep the gear lever in the neutral position. On Citroën models with hydraulic suspension (BX, CX, XM, etc), if the engine isn't running the brakes won't work.

■ If the car being towed has automatic transmission, the gear lever should be moved to the 'N' position. The manufacturer often recommends that you don't exceed a certain speed or distance when towing – check your car's handbook for details. Ideally, a car with automatic transmission should be towed with the driven wheels off the ground.

■ An 'On-tow' notice should be displayed at the rear of the car on tow.

■ Make sure that both drivers know details of the route to be taken before setting off.

■ Before moving away, the tow car should be driven slowly forwards to take up any slack in the tow-rope.

■ The driver of the car on tow should try to keep the tow-rope tight at all times – by gently using the brakes if necessary.

■ Drive smoothly at all times, especially when moving away from a standstill.

■ Allow plenty of time to slow down and stop, especially when approaching junctions and traffic queues.

What to do if you've locked yourself out of your car

If you've locked your keys inside your car, and you can't easily get hold of a spare set, you'll have to find a way to break in.

The best option is to call one of the motoring organisations, who are likely to be able to get into a car with minimal damage. Unfortunately, it's quite likely that some damage will be caused whether you try to break in yourself, or whether you leave it to the 'professionals'.

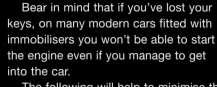

RIGHT Make sure you keep a record of your car key number – sometimes the master key has a numbered identification tag like this

Bear in mind that if you've lost your keys, on many modern cars fitted with immobilisers you won't be able to start the engine even if you manage to get into the car.

The following will help to minimise the inconvenience if you do manage to lock yourself out of your car:

- Carry a spare set of keys.
- Make sure that you have a note of the key number and, where applicable, the immobiliser code number (these are often supplied on a 'key card' when the car is new) – these will make it easier to obtain a new key.
- Never leave the key in the car, even if you've just popped into your house. It's very easy to become distracted and forget where you left the key.

Jump starting

If you have a flat battery, you can start the car by using jump leads to connect the flat battery to a charged one, whether or not it's fitted to another vehicle. Here's a guide to jump starting, assuming that the charged battery is fitted to another vehicle.

Warning: Be wary when jump starting cars with engine management systems – careless jump starting, particularly if the leads are allowed to spark, can cause damage to the car's electronic components. Some cars, such as certain BMWs, are fitted with special connectors to allow jump starting, and on these cars the jump leads should only be connected to the special terminals provided. It's a good idea to read your car's handbook carefully to see if there are any special recommendations to be observed when using jump leads. If in doubt, call one of the breakdown services, as they will have the equipment to get your car running without any risk of damage.

Jump starting a car

1 Position the vehicles so that you can connect the batteries together using the jump leads, but don't let the vehicles touch. Switch off the ignition and all electrical equipment on both vehicles, make sure that handbrakes are applied, and make sure that the gears are in neutral (manual gearbox), or 'P' on automatic transmission models.

2 Connect one end of the RED jump lead to the positive (+) terminal of the flat battery. Don't let the other end of the jump lead touch any vehicle metal.

3 Connect the other end of the RED lead to the positive (+) terminal of the fully charged battery.

4 Connect one end of the BLACK jump lead to the negative (–) terminal of the fully charged battery.

5 Connect the other end of the BLACK jump lead to a bolt or metal bracket, well away from the battery, on the engine block of the vehicle to be started.

6 Make sure that the jump leads can't come into contact with any moving parts of either engine, then start the engine of the vehicle with the fully charged battery and run it at a fast tickover.

7 Start the engine of the vehicle with the flat battery, and make sure that it's running properly.

8 Stop the engine of the vehicle with the fully charged battery, then disconnect the jump leads. Disconnect the BLACK lead first – from the vehicle with the flat battery, and then from the vehicle with the fully charged battery; then disconnect the RED lead – from the vehicle with the fully charged battery first, then from the vehicle with the flat battery.

9 Keep the use of electrical equipment to a minimum, and remember that it will take some time for the alternator to charge the flat battery. Don't stop the engine too soon, and try not to stall it whilst driving.

Know
your car

Engine

Most modern car engines run on either petrol or diesel fuel, and are known as internal combustion engines because the fuel is burnt inside the engine to produce power. Liquid Petroleum Gas (LPG) is now becoming commonplace as a fuel, and cars which run on LPG use modified petrol engines.

Although today's engines may at first sight seem complicated, in fact, if the designers of the first internal combustion engines were able to examine the engines fitted to even the most sophisticated modern cars they might be surprised how little has changed. Modern materials and computer technology have made engines lighter, quieter and far more efficient, but the mechanical components at the heart of the engine have changed very little.

How does it work?

A car engine is a machine that converts chemical energy – stored in hydrocarbon compounds contained in the fuel – into mechanical energy in the form of motion. In order for the fuel to burn, it must be mixed with air, and the air is sucked into the engine through an air filter, which is there to stop dirt and other contaminants from getting inside where they could cause serious damage to the engine's moving parts.

The engine consists of a number of cylinders – anything from two (quite rare) to 16 (in the most advanced and expensive high-performance cars). The most common number for everyday cars is four. Each cylinder has a piston inside, and is sealed at the top by the cylinder head. The cylinders are located in the cylinder block, the largest single component of the engine.

The cylinder head contains inlet and exhaust valves. The valves allow the air/fuel mixture into the cylinder, and burnt gases out into the exhaust system. The valves are opened and closed by a camshaft, which is driven from the crankshaft, usually by a belt (known as the 'cam belt' or 'timing belt') or sometimes a chain.

The air/fuel mixture is burnt inside a small area at the top of the cylinder called a combustion

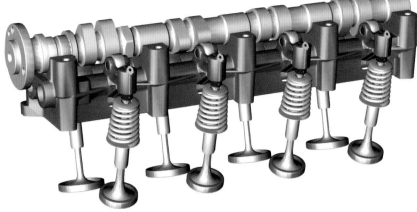

chamber and, depending on the engine design, the combustion chamber may be located either in the cylinder head or in the top of the piston. In order to burn, the air and fuel must be mixed together, and this happens either in the inlet tract, which is separated from the combustion chamber by the inlet valve(s), or in the combustion chamber itself.

Almost all engines produced since the early 1990s (both petrol and diesel) use fuel injection, which means that the fuel is injected under pressure into the engine. The fuel is injected either into the inlet tract, where it's mixed with the air and then fed to the combustion chamber through the inlet valve(s); or, on the latest Direct Injection (DI) engines, it is injected directly into the combustion chamber.

ABOVE LEFT A typical engine cylinder block – in this case from a 4-cylinder BMW engine

ABOVE The valves are opened and closed by a camshaft, which pushes against the pressure of the valve springs, visible on this Mercedes A-Class engine

As each piston moves up its cylinder, it compresses the air/fuel mixture, and when the mixture ignites and burns it expands very quickly and pushes the piston back down the cylinder. The bottom of each piston is fastened to a connecting rod, which is in turn fastened to the crankshaft. As the pistons move up and down, the connecting rods push the crankshaft round. The crankshaft carries all the power from the engine to the transmission, which drives the car's wheels.

In petrol engines the air/fuel mixture is ignited by a spark from a spark plug, but in diesel engines the air/fuel mixture is compressed to a much higher pressure than that in petrol engines, which causes the temperature in the combustion chamber to rise very quickly, igniting the mixture without a spark.

LEFT In a direct injection engine (a diesel engine in this case), fuel is injected directly into the combustion chamber

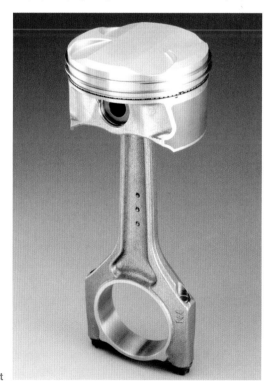

LEFT In a petrol engine, the air/fuel mixture is ignited in the combustion chamber by a spark plug

RIGHT The piston/ connecting rod assemblies transmit the energy created by burning the air/fuel mixture to the crankshaft

The four-stroke cycle

Most car engines are four-stroke, which means that each piston moves up and down twice (two up-strokes, and two down-strokes, making four strokes), to produce one pulse of power. In a four-stroke engine, the four strokes are:

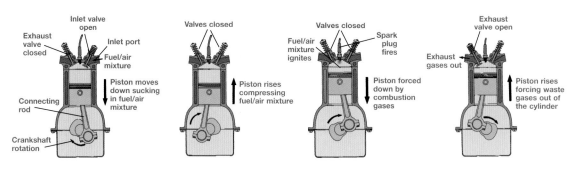

1 Intake
The piston moves down the cylinder, sucking air/fuel mixture from the inlet manifold into the cylinder and combustion chamber through the inlet valve.

2 Compression
The valves are closed and the piston moves up the cylinder, compressing the mixture until it's ignited in the combustion chamberat the top of the stroke.

3 Power
The valves stay closed as the piston is pushed down the cylinder due to the expansion of the burning mixture.

4 Exhaust
The piston moves back up the cylinder (because of the momentum produced during the power stroke), and the burnt gases are pushed out through the open exhaust valve. The cycle then starts again, with another intake stroke.

The oil system

Oil is the engine's blood. If the oil is neglected, the moving components inside the engine will wear, and will eventually seize. The engine needs oil for two reasons – to act as a lubricant, and to help to keep it cool.

RIGHT A cutaway view of a typical oil filter. The arrows show the flow of oil from the engine, through the filter element and back into the engine

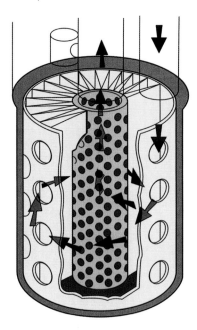

Many of the metal components inside the engine move at very high speed within just a few fractions of a millimetre of each other, and they rely on a thin film of oil between them to prevent the components from rubbing together. If the components are allowed to rub together, they will very quickly overheat and seize up, which can wreck the engine.

When the engine is stopped, the oil is stored in a tray called the sump, bolted to the bottom of the cylinder block. When the engine is running, the oil is pumped from the sump to all the moving parts of the engine through small passages in the cylinder block and cylinder head. The oil pump is driven by the engine, usually from the crankshaft. As the oil circulates through the engine it picks up tiny particles of dirt and, as the engine wears, tiny particles of metal, which would eventually damage the engine's moving parts. The oil passes through a filter that catches these small particles, and the oil filter is one of the most critical parts of the engine. Eventually this filter starts to clog up, and the oil can't flow through as easily, so it must be changed whenever the engine oil is changed at the recommended service intervals.

Regular checking and servicing of the oil system will make sure that the engine has a long and happy life. If the oil level is allowed to become low, or if the oil and filter aren't changed at the recommended intervals, the engine will wear more quickly and the fuel consumption will increase.

The cooling system

The cooling system is vital, because it stops the engine overheating. It also keeps the engine at an efficient working temperature, and provides heat for the heater inside the car. The cooling system consists of a radiator (mounted in front of the engine), a coolant (water) pump (mounted on the engine), a cooling fan (which cools the radiator), a thermostat (which controls the flow of coolant to the radiator), and an expansion tank (which allows the coolant to expand as it heats up). On all modern engines the cooling system is pressurised, which allows the coolant to reach temperatures above the boiling point of water without the coolant turning to steam.

The car's heating system is really part of the engine cooling system, and consists of a heater matrix (a mini radiator), a blower motor, a control panel, and various flaps and air ducts inside the car.

The coolant is made up of a mixture of water and antifreeze. The antifreeze is used to raise the boiling point of water (to help prevent it turning to steam) and also to prevent the metal components inside the engine from rusting. Many cars now have 'sealed-for-life' cooling systems, which means that the coolant should never need changing, but it's considered good practice to renew the coolant every few years.

The coolant pump is usually driven by a belt from the engine, often by the timing belt. The

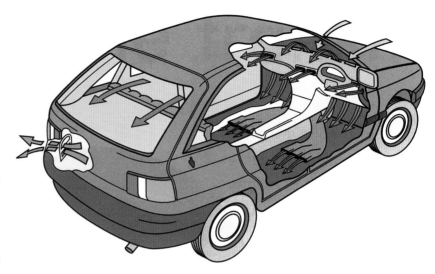

ABOVE A car's heating system draws cool air from outside the car over a heater matrix and distributes the warm air through air ducts inside the car. Arrows show direction of air flow

Cooling system layout

1 Engine cylinder block
2 Radiator
3 Expansion tank
4 Heater matrix
5 Inlet manifold
6 Bleed screws
7 Coolant pump
8 Cooling fan switch

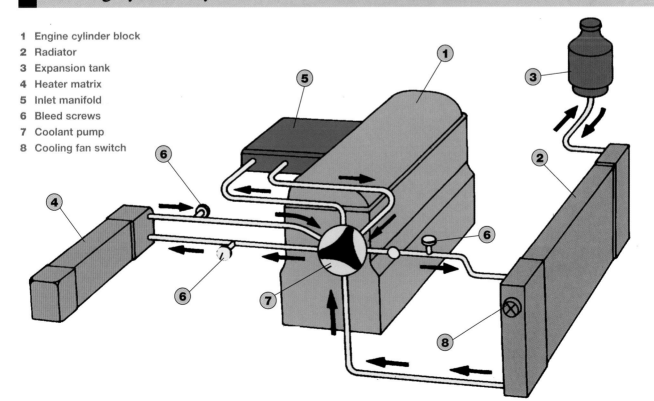

Engine jargon explained

Timing belt

Most modern engines have a timing belt (or 'cam belt'), although some may have a timing chain instead. The timing belt is driven by the engine's crankshaft, and provides the drive to the camshafts, which open and close the engine's valves. The timing belt is one of the most critical parts of the engine, and if it fails, expensive engine damage can be caused. It's therefore very important to make sure that the timing belt is renewed at the manufacturer's recommended intervals. On many engines, it's recommended that some or all of the timing belt pulleys should be renewed whenever a new belt is fitted.

16-valve (or multi-valve) engines

Most older car engines have one inlet valve and one exhaust valve per cylinder – ie, two valves per cylinder. Many modern engines have three, four, or in a few cases even five valves per cylinder, although the most common arrangement is four. An engine with four valves per cylinder has two inlet valves and two exhaust valves for each cylinder – so a four-cylinder engine would be a '16-valve' engine. Using multiple valves helps to improve engine efficiency because it improves the flow of the air/fuel mixture into the cylinders, and the flow of the exhaust gases out of the cylinders.

Double-Overhead-Camshaft (DOHC or TOHC) engines

Double-overhead-camshaft (or 'twin-cam') engines have two camshafts, one operating the exhaust valves, and one operating the inlet valves. Multi-valve engines are almost always double-overhead-camshaft engines.

Variable Valve Timing (VVT)

Variable valve timing makes it possible to vary the exact instant at which the valves open and close whilst the engine is running. The system is controlled by the engine management system according to the engine's operating conditions. Varying the valve timing improves engine performance and efficiency because it allows the flow of air/fuel mixture into the cylinders, and the flow of exhaust gases out of the cylinders, to be varied to suit the engine's requirements under different conditions.

Diesel engines

Most models of car are now available with a diesel engine, and many modern diesel engines run just as smoothly as petrol engines. Diesel engines use diesel fuel instead of petrol, and the big difference in the way petrol and diesel engines work is the way in which the fuel burns. A petrol engine needs a spark plug to ignite the fuel with a spark, but in a diesel engine the fuel ignites by itself due to the high pressure and temperature inside the combustion chamber. As diesel engines rely on a high temperature to ignite the fuel, when they're first started from cold they use 'glow plugs' to heat the mixture to a high enough temperature to ignite. Generally, diesel engines use less fuel than petrol engines, and they're considered to produce less pollution.

coolant is pumped around passages inside the engine, collecting heat from the engine components as if flows through. The hot coolant then passes from the engine to the radiator, where the air forced through the radiator as the car moves forward cools it. The cooling fan draws cool air over the radiator when the speed of the car is too low (or the car is stopped), of if the air temperature is too high to give enough cooling. The cooling fan is usually electrically operated, although some older cars may have a belt-driven fan.

The thermostat is normally fitted inside a housing attached to the engine. Its job is to allow the engine to warm up quickly by restricting the flow of coolant to the radiator when the engine is cold. It also regulates the normal operating temperature of the engine.

A pressure cap is fitted to the cooling system, either on the expansion tank or on the radiator. The pressure cap effectively pressurises the cooling system as the temperature rises, which raises the boiling point of the coolant. The cap acts as a safety valve by venting steam or hot coolant if the pressure rises above a certain level.

Most cars have a temperature gauge which

The thermostat

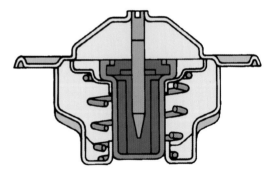

COLD – VALVE CLOSED

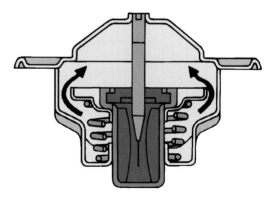

HOT – VALVE OPEN

allows the driver to keep an eye on the engine temperature. It's a good idea to make a mental note of where the needle usually sits, so that you will know if anything is abnormal. If the needle moves into the red section, stop the engine as soon as possible, as engine overheating can cause serious and expensive damage.

Auxiliary drivebelts

Auxiliary drivebelts are usually driven by a pulley on the end of the crankshaft, and their job is to drive the engine ancillaries, such as the alternator, power steering pump and air conditioning compressor, and, on some cars, the coolant pump. One belt may drive all the ancillaries, or several separate belts may be used.

On diesel-engined cars, the fuel injection pump may be driven by a drivebelt, or by the engine timing belt. Diesel engines may also have a belt-driven vacuum pump to provide vacuum for the brake servo.

Drivebelt checking is part of the maintenance schedule on most cars, and you'll almost certainly have to renew the drivebelt(s) at some stage if you keep the car for any length of time.

Do's and don'ts to keep your engine in tip-top condition

ABOVE Gone are the days of the simple 'fanbelt'! On many modern cars a single drivebelt is used to drive all the engine ancillaries

DO

 Check the engine oil level every week, and before a long journey.

 Change the engine oil and filter at the intervals recommended by the car manufacturer, or more often if you can afford to.

 Check the coolant level and the drivebelt(s) regularly.

 Take the car out for a long run occasionally, if you normally only use it for short journeys.

 Stop immediately if the oil pressure warning light comes on when you're driving – it's not an oil level warning light, and you'll wreck the engine if you don't stop very quickly!

DON'T

 Warm the engine up by leaving the car parked with the engine running – it's better just to start the engine and drive off straight away, even in winter.

 Warm the engine up by revving it more than normal.

 Rev the engine more than you need to until the temperature gauge has reached its normal position.

 carry on driving the car if you know the engine is overheating.

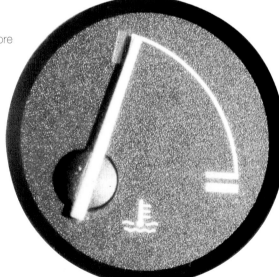

Fuel systems

The fuel system's job is to provide the engine with the fuel it needs, and to control the amount of air and fuel burnt by the engine to produce power as efficiently as possible. The fuel system consists of the fuel tank, a fuel pump and filter (to stop any dirt from the tank reaching the fuel injection components), the fuel injection system itself, and the fuel lines that connect all the components together. The fuel injection system is usually controlled by an engine management system, and modern fuel systems are extremely reliable.

Different types of fuel

The two main types of fuel for cars are petrol and diesel. LPG (Liquefied Petroleum Gas) is becoming more common, and there are now some electric cars in use, mainly in city centres.

Petrol and diesel fuel are produced from crude oil. Because petrol is now such an important fuel, it's production has become much more efficient and the amount of petrol obtained from one barrel of crude oil has gone up significantly from the days when crude oil was first discovered. It's now possible to get nearly half a barrel of petrol from one barrel of crude oil. Half of the crude oil produced is used to make petrol!

Once petrol and diesel fuel have been refined from crude oil, they're treated with various additives and detergents to make them suitable for use in car engines.

The reserves of natural crude oil are beginning to run out, and it's widely believed that they'll be exhausted completely within the next few decades. Most car manufacturers are trying to build more fuel-efficient engines, in an attempt to eke out the oil reserves for longer. A number of companies are also carrying out research to develop alternative forms of power, such as electricity and hydrogen fuel, and there are a number of hybrid-power cars on the roads which use both petrol engines and electric motors.

Petrol

In recent years, it's been realised that petrol-engine exhaust fumes cause a significant pollution problem throughout the world. All car engines are now fitted with systems to cut down harmful exhaust emissions, and the petrol itself is 'cleaner'.

Diesel

Diesel cars are more fuel-efficient than petrol-engined cars, and diesel engines produce less harmful exhaust emissions than petrol engines, although they produce more smoke particles.

LPG (Liquefied Petroleum Gas)

LPG is a mixture of liquefied petroleum gases obtained from crude oil. It is stored as a liquid in a pressurised container, and is released to form a vapour before being burnt by the engine. Although a conventional internal combustion engine is used (similar to a petrol engine), a special pressurised fuel tank and modified fuel system components are fitted.

An engine running on LPG is less fuel-efficient than a similar engine running on petrol, but the exhaust emissions are much cleaner.

Because LPG is produced from crude oil, sources of LPG are likely to run out, so although it is more environmentally friendly it isn't a long-term alternative to petrol.

Electricity

An electric car is fitted with a number of batteries to drive an electric motor that powers the car.

Although electric cars themselves cause very little pollution and are cheap to run, at present the batteries they use are very heavy and need to be recharged often – which means that electric cars

LEFT LPG fuel is becoming more widely available, and several manufacturers now produce 'bi-fuel' cars which will run on both petrol and LPG

can travel relatively small distances between 'refuelling' (recharging) stops. The power stations that produce the electricity may also be causing pollution, so the electric car may not be as 'green' as it first seems.

Most of the large car manufacturers are carrying out research into electric cars to improve their performance and practicality, so they should become more widespread in the future.

BELOW Electric cars, such as this adapted Peugeot 106, are still few and far between, but are ideal for use on short commuter runs in cities

Fuel system jargon explained

Air filter

Air is sucked into an engine when the pistons move down the cylinders, creating suction. If the air contained dirt, insects or any other contamination, it would be sucked straight into the engine, possibly causing serious damage to the components. To prevent this, a filter is used to filter out any dirt before it can enter the engine. The air filter must be renewed regularly, otherwise it will become blocked and won't allow enough air into the engine, so air filter renewal is always an important item on the service schedule.

Carburettors

Before fuel injection systems were commonplace, carburettors were fitted to most cars. In the early 1990s carburettors were phased out in most of Europe and the US when exhaust emissions became an important consideration, and the use of fuel injection systems – which allow fine control of the air/fuel mixture – became the only way of meeting the tightening regulations.

A carburettor's job is to mix the fuel and air before it's fed to the engine's cylinders. It does this by using the flow of air sucked into the engine to draw fuel through finely calibrated passages in the carburettor body into a tube called a venturi, where the air and fuel mix before passing into the engine.

Direct Injection (DI) engines

Both petrol and diesel engines may have either 'direct' or 'indirect' injection. On an indirect-injection diesel engine, the fuel injector pumps the fuel into a 'swirl chamber' in the cylinder head above the combustion chamber, which swirls the fuel around to mix it with the air. On an indirect-injection petrol engine, each fuel injector pumps fuel into the inlet tract, where it mixes with air before passing through the inlet valve into the combustion chamber.

On a direct-injection (DI) engine, whether petrol or diesel, the fuel injector pumps the fuel directly into the combustion chamber, where it is mixed with the air. The recent improvements in diesel engine technology mean that direct injection is now the most efficient option, and direct injection is also becoming more common in petrol engines.

Turbochargers and superchargers

An engine without a supercharger or turbocharger is known as a 'normally aspirated' engine, which relies on the movement of the pistons down the cylinders creating suction to draw air in. On an engine with a turbocharger or a supercharger, air is forced into the engine by a 'pump'. Because the amount of power an engine produces depends on the quantity of air/fuel mixture it can burn, it follows that the more air/fuel that can be forced into the engine, the more power will be produced. Both turbochargers and superchargers act as air pumps, and the difference between them is that a turbocharger is driven by the engine exhaust gases passing over the vanes of a turbine, whereas a supercharger is mechanically driven from the engine's crankshaft, usually by a belt but sometimes through a series of gears. Turbochargers are commonly used on diesel engines to increase power.

Common-rail diesel injection system

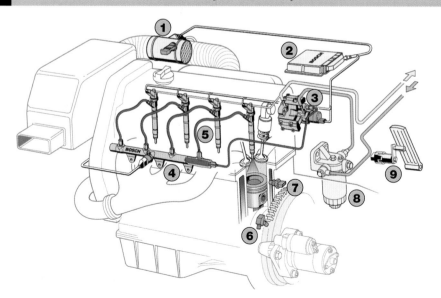

1 Air mass meter
2 Engine ECU
3 High Pressure Pump
4 Common Rail
5 Injectors
6 Engine Speed Sensor
7 Coolant Tempreture Sensor
8 Filter
9 Accelerator Pedal Sensor

Fuel injection systems (petrol engines)

All modern petrol engines are fitted with fuel injection systems. There are two basic types, single-point and multi-point. A single-point system has a single fuel injector, which sprays fuel into the inlet manifold where it's mixed with air before passing through the engine's inlet valves into the cylinders. A multi-point system works in exactly the same way, except that a separate fuel injector is used for each cylinder, which allows much finer control of the air/fuel mixture than a single-point system. With a multi-point system, the air/fuel mixture can be varied for each individual cylinder, maximising efficiency and minimising exhaust emissions.

Diesel fuel systems

On a diesel engine, a separate fuel injector is used for each of the engine's cylinders. The biggest difference between petrol and diesel injection systems is the pressure under which the fuel is injected. Extremely high pressures are used in modern diesel engines – much higher than the pressure used in petrol engines.

Various different types of injection system are used on diesel engines, but in the most common 'conventional' system an engine-driven fuel injection pump pumps fuel to each of the fuel injectors, or to a 'common rail'.

On a common-rail diesel engine, all the fuel injectors are fed from the same pressurised fuel reservoir (rail), whereas on a conventional engine each injector receives its own separate fuel supply direct from the pump. A common-rail system allows finer control of the engine, giving improved efficiency, and this is the system being used on more and more modern cars.

Some diesel engines use 'unit injectors' where each injector incorporates a high-pressure fuel pump as well as a conventional injector. The advantage of this system is that the fuel is under low pressure until it reaches the injectors, which means that no high-pressure fuel lines are needed.

Glow plugs are fitted to diesel engines to help start the engine from cold and to reduce smoke immediately after start-up. A diesel engine relies on a high temperature in the cylinder to ignite the air/fuel mixture – a cold engine, combined with cold air being drawn into the engine, won't give a high enough temperature. The glow plugs are electrical heater elements (called glow plugs because they glow red hot), and usually (though not always) one glow plug is fitted to each

Diesel fuel system

Arrows show direction of fuel flow

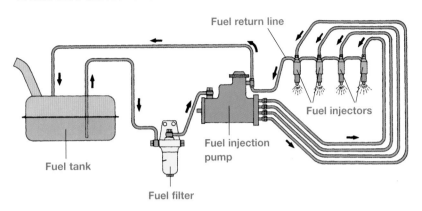

Fuel return line

Fuel injectors

Fuel injection pump

Fuel tank

Fuel filter

cylinder. On most modern diesel engines an electronic control unit controls the glow plugs automatically. The glow plugs are switched on when the ignition key is turned to the 'start' position, and a warning light on the instrument panel comes on to show that they're working. The warning light goes out when the glow plugs have heated up enough to start the engine.

BELOW Glow plugs (arrowed), so called because they glow red hot, are used to ignite the air/fuel mixture when the engine is cold

Ignition
systems

The ignition system produces the sparks used to ignite the air/fuel mixture in a petrol engine (diesel engines don't have an ignition system). The ignition coil transforms the low voltage electricity from the battery into high-voltage electricity, which is sent along the HT (High Tension) leads to the spark plugs. The spark plugs are screwed into the cylinder head, and produce sparks inside the combustion chambers.

Ignition timing

The exact instant at which the air/fuel mixture inside each cylinder is ignited is critical, and has an important effect on how the engine performs. The instant at which the mixture ignites in each cylinder depends on when the spark plug produces a spark to ignite it. The timing of the spark is known as ignition timing, and this can be controlled very accurately by the engine management system. On most modern systems the ignition timing is varied constantly, and the timing for each of the engine's cylinders is controlled individually, which helps to maximise the efficiency of the engine.

Distributor-based ignition systems

Until the introduction of electronic engine management systems, a distributor was the main component of the ignition system, controlling the coil and the ignition timing and distributing the high-tension (HT) voltage from the coil to the spark plugs. Nowadays, if a distributor is used at all its sole job is to distribute the HT voltage to the spark plugs.

A 'rotor arm' inside the distributor is driven by the engine, and rotates inside the distributor cap. The coil is connected to the rotor arm, which spins past a series of contacts – one for each of the engine's cylinders. As the rotor arm passes each contact in the cap, a pulse from the ignition coil jumps the small gap between the rotor arm and the contact (they don't actually touch) and then passes down the HT lead to the appropriate spark plug.

Distributors are now rare, and most modern engines have a distributorless ignition system.

ABOVE A direct ignition system (DIS) is used on the MINI engine. The DIS module (arrowed) is connected directly to the spark plugs by the HT leads

BELOW Spark plugs are used to ignite the air/fuel mixture in a petrol engine, and must be kept in good condition to enable the engine to run efficiently

Direct ignition systems (or 'distributorless' ignition systems)

A direct ignition system (sometimes known as DIS) does not have a distributor. The HT leads run directly from the coil to the spark plugs – the coil has a connection for each of the engine's cylinders – and the ignition timing is controlled by the engine management system.

Some engines actually have a separate coil for each cylinder, and on these systems the coils are often fitted directly above the spark plugs, which means that long HT leads aren't needed.

Spark plugs

Spark plugs are fitted to petrol engines, and their job is to ignite the air/fuel mixture in the cylinders at the correct instant.

When the ignition system sends a voltage down the HT lead to the spark plug, the high voltage causes a spark to jump between the spark plug centre electrode and the earth electrode(s). The spark ignites the explosive air/fuel mixture, which expands, pushing the piston down the cylinder.

The 'spark plug gap' (the gap between the earth electrode(s) and the centre electrode) can be adjusted to suit a particular engine. The size of the gap is very important, because it controls the way the air/fuel mixture burns. Some spark plugs have more than one earth electrode.

Engine management

A modern engine fitted with an engine management system gives greater reliability, better fuel economy, better performance, and needs less maintenance than an engine without engine management. Engine management systems are essential to enable modern engines to meet the strict exhaust emissions regulations.

```
RPM        0     22  °C
CO    %  vol      3.33
C02   %  vol     12.48
HC   ppm vol       480
02    %  vol      0.32
λ     0.903
MENU         TIMING        MORE
```

How does engine management work?

An engine management system is controlled by an electronic control unit (ECU), which is connected to various sensors and actuators fitted around the engine. The sensors monitor the engine operating conditions and produce electrical signals that are sent to the ECU. The ECU processes all the information from the sensors and is able to tell exactly what conditions the engine is running under. The ECU has various engine 'maps' stored in its memory, and the maps provide details of how much fuel is required and the optimum ignition timing (or injection timing in the case of diesel engines) for given conditions. Based on the information it receives from the sensors, the ECU sends signals to various components such as the fuel injectors, the coil (petrol engines), the engine idle speed control valve and the emission control systems, to control the engine.

An engine management system enables extremely fine control of the engine. The ECU performs hundreds of calculations per second, constantly varying the signals that it sends to the various systems it controls so that the engine is able to function as efficiently and smoothly as possible.

Diagnostic systems

Engine management systems usually have an on-board diagnostic system (or self-diagnostic system), which is used to store details of any faults. If a component is faulty, the system stores a fault code in the ECU and will usually switch on a warning light on the instrument panel to indicate that a fault is present. The fault codes indicate which component or system is at fault, and can be read using special diagnostic equipment such as a fault code reader. This allows faults to be traced quickly and easily.

Emissions
control systems

When the air/fuel mixture is burnt inside the engine, exhaust gases are produced. Known as exhaust emissions, these pass through the car's exhaust system out into the atmosphere, causing pollution. There are strict regulations restricting the release of such gases, which means that all cars must have emissions control systems fitted.

What systems are fitted?

All modern engines are designed with low emissions in mind, and using engine management systems helps to reduce emissions by giving much better control of the engine. This means that the engine burns the air/fuel mixture more efficiently, to produce less pollution.

Various emissions control systems are fitted to reduce emissions further, in order to meet the strict regulations in force in most countries.

Crankcase ventilation system

Instead of releasing the oil fumes produced inside the engine directly into the atmosphere, a crankcase ventilation system is used. This recirculates the fumes by drawing them into the engine's combustion chambers, where they're mixed with fresh air/fuel mixture and burnt.

Crankcase ventilation system

Idle & part load flow

Full load flow

1 Air cleaner
2 Valve
3 Orifice
4 Inlet manifold
5 Ventilation manifold
6 Crankcase

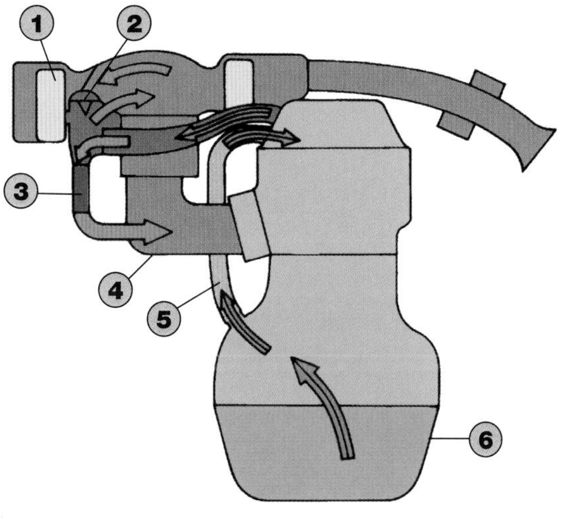

Catalytic converter

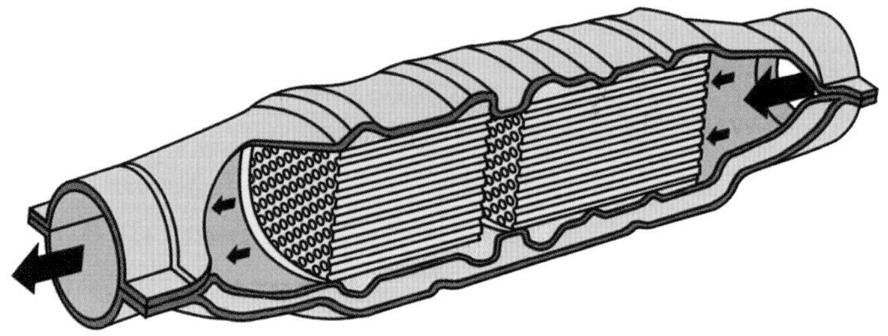

Carbon Monoxide (CO)
Hydrocarbons (HC)
Nitrogen Oxides (NO_2)

Carbon Dioxide (CO_2)
Water (H_2O)
Nitrogen (N)

Catalytic converter

All modern petrol-engined cars and most modern diesels are fitted with catalytic converters. The catalytic converter is fitted into the exhaust system under the car, and consists of a steel canister containing a honeycomb material coated with a substance called a catalyst, which speeds up a chemical change without being altered itself. The exhaust gases pass over the honeycomb, where the catalyst accelerates the conversion of the harmful gases into harmless gases and water vapour.

On most petrol-engined cars fitted with a catalytic converter, an oxygen (or 'Lambda') sensor is fitted to the exhaust system. This is used by the engine management system to

Closed loop catalytic converter system

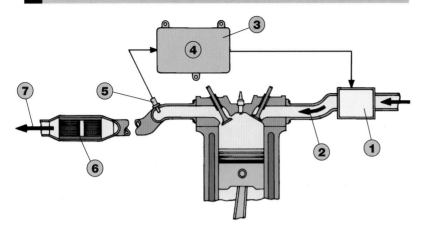

1 Fuel system
2 Air/Fuel mixture
3 Engine management
4 Electronic control unit
5 Oxygen sensor
6 Catalytic converter
7 Exhaust gases

control the air/fuel mixture. If the mixture is kept within certain limits, the catalyst can work at its maximum efficiency. The oxygen sensor sends the engine management system details of how much oxygen is in the exhaust gas, and this is used to automatically control the air/fuel mixture.

After a number of years the catalytic converter will have to be renewed, because the catalyst inside will deteriorate with age.

Exhaust gas recirculation (EGR)

This system diverts some of the exhaust gas from the exhaust system back into the engine. The recirculated exhaust gas is drawn into the cylinders with fresh air/fuel mixture, and burnt. This reduces the amount of unburned fuel passing into the exhaust system.

Fuel evaporative control system (EVAP)

This system is only used on petrol engines. Instead of allowing fuel vapour from the tank to vent into the atmosphere when the engine is stopped, the vapour is passed to a charcoal canister (the charcoal absorbs the fuel vapour). When the engine is running, the vapour is drawn into the engine and burnt. As the vapour is drawn from the canister, fresh air is fed in, cleaning the charcoal.

Pulse air system (or 'air injection system')

This system is becoming less common because of the improvement in the control and efficiency of catalytic converters. Fresh air is pumped into the exhaust manifold through tubes, and this increases the temperature of the exhaust gases. This in turn causes the catalyst to warm up more quickly, making sure that it reaches maximum efficiency as soon as possible after starting the engine.

Fuel Evaporative control system (EVAP)

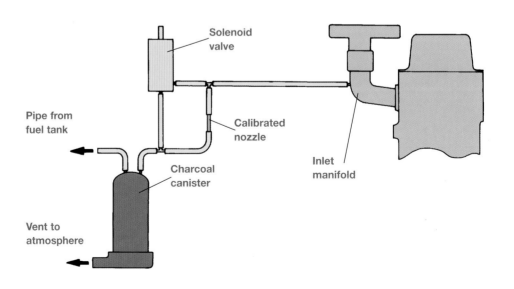

Transmission

'Transmission' is the term used for the group of components that transmit power from the engine to the car's wheels. The components used depend on whether the car has the front wheels, rear wheels, or all four wheels driven. As well as the manual or automatic gearbox itself, components include a clutch (manual transmission only), a differential, driveshafts, and, on rear-wheel-drive and four-wheel-drive cars, a propeller shaft.

Different transmission layouts

Typical front-wheel drive layout

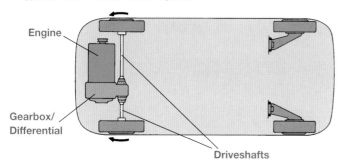

Typical four-wheel drive layout

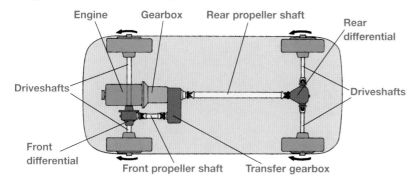

Typical rear-wheel drive layout

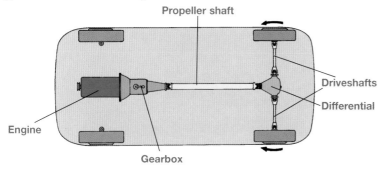

Clutch

The clutch allows power to be transferred smoothly from the engine to the transmission when moving away from a standstill and when changing gear. The clutch has five main components – the friction disc, the pressure plate, the diaphragm spring, the cover, and the release bearing.

The friction disc slides freely back and forth on a shaft at the front of the gearbox, known as the gearbox input shaft. When the friction disc turns, it turns the input shaft. The friction disc is held firmly in place between the engine flywheel (a large metal plate attached to the engine's crankshaft) and the clutch pressure plate by a diaphragm spring pushing against the latter. The friction disc has friction material fitted to both sides.

The diaphragm spring is mounted on pins in the cover, and is held in place by thin metal fulcrum rings built into the cover.

The release bearing slides on a guide sleeve at the front of the gearbox, and the release arm – which pivots inside the gearbox casing – moves the bearing. The release arm is operated by the clutch cable, or on some cars by a hydraulic system.

When the clutch pedal is pushed down, the release bearing moves to operate the diaphragm spring. The diaphragm spring moves, and allows the pressure plate to move away from the flywheel, which releases the pressure on the friction disc and allows the friction disc to move away from the flywheel, 'releasing' the clutch. When the clutch is released, no power is transferred from the engine to the gearbox, making it possible for the driver to change gear. As the clutch pedal moves back up, the whole process is reversed, and the pressure plate forces the friction disc back against the flywheel, engaging the clutch and again transferring power from the engine to the gearbox.

Clutch assembly

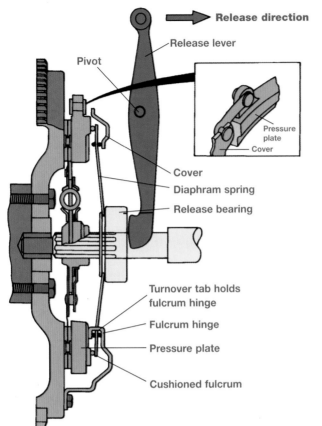

Release direction

Release lever

Pivot

Pressure plate

Cover

Cover

Diaphram spring

Release bearing

Turnover tab holds fulcrum hinge

Fulcrum hinge

Pressure plate

Cushioned fulcrum

Manual gearbox

A manual gearbox allows the driver to select the best gear to suit the car's speed and the road conditions.

On front-wheel-drive cars, the gearbox usually has two shafts inside, the input shaft and the output shaft. The shafts run next to each other,

and the gears on the two shafts are in constant mesh. The gears on the input shaft are permanently fixed to the shaft, but the gears on the output shaft are free to turn (so the output shaft can turn whilst the gears on it stay still).

When a gear is selected, a lever moves a sliding synchromesh hub along the output shaft, which locks the appropriate gear to the shaft. One synchromesh assembly is fitted for each gear. The job of each assembly is to allow smooth, quiet gear engagement by making sure that the gear is spinning at the same speed as the output shaft when the two are locked together. Drive is transmitted from the output shaft to the differential, which is built into the gearbox casing.

Although some rear-wheel-drive cars have a similar gearbox to the one described previously for front-wheel-drive cars, most have a gearbox which contains three shafts – the input shaft, the output shaft, and a 'layshaft'. The input shaft runs in line with the output shaft, and both the input and output shaft gears are in constant mesh with the gears on the layshaft. The gears on the input and output shafts are permanently fixed to the shafts, but the gears on the layshaft are free to turn (so the layshaft can turn whilst the gears stay still). When a gear is selected, a lever moves a synchromesh hub along the layshaft, which locks the appropriate gear to the shaft. Drive is transmitted from the output shaft to a propeller shaft, which transmits drive to the differential.

Various types of gearbox are used on four-wheel-drive cars, but the most common type is similar to the rear-wheel-drive type described previously.

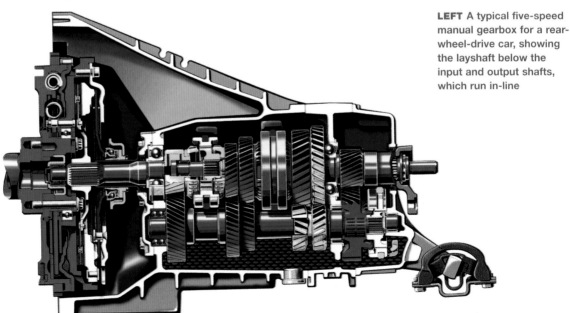

LEFT A typical five-speed manual gearbox for a rear-wheel-drive car, showing the layshaft below the input and output shafts, which run in-line

Automatic transmission assembly

Automatic transmission

There are two basic types of automatic transmission. A conventional automatic transmission uses a torque converter and a gearbox, and the other type, used mainly on smaller cars, is a Continuously Variable Transmission (CVT). With either type, gear changing during normal driving is automatic.

Conventional automatic transmission

In a conventional automatic transmission, the torque converter acts as a coupling between the engine and transmission, taking the place of the clutch in a manual transmission. The torque converter transmits the drive to an 'epicyclic' gearbox, which provides several forward gears and reverse gear, depending on which components of the gearbox are held stationary or allowed to turn. The gearbox components are held stationary or released by hydraulic brakes and clutches. A fluid pump built into the transmission provides the hydraulic pressure to operate the brakes and clutches, which are controlled by an electronic control unit. An output shaft transmits power to the differential (front-wheel-drive cars) or the propeller shaft (rear-wheel-drive cars).

Continuously variable transmission (CVT)

Several different types of CVT have been produced, but they all work in a similar way. The input shaft drives a cone-shaped pulley, which in turn drives a belt (usually made of metal). The belt drives a second cone-shaped pulley, which is

ABOVE An automatic transmission is a complex unit, as this cutaway view of a BMW 6-speed example shows

linked to the output shaft. The gear ratio can be varied constantly by allowing the belt to run on different parts of the two pulleys – this is done using a hydraulic control system that moves one half of each pulley towards or away from its other half.

Differential

When a car turns a corner, the wheels on the outside of the turn must travel further (and so faster) than the wheels on the inside. If no differential is fitted, the driven wheel on the outside of the turn will try to resist turning because it's only able to turn at the same speed as the wheel on the inside. To overcome this problem a differential is used to allow the wheels to rotate at different speeds.

The differential is made up of a crownwheel, a cage, a cross-shaft, two sun gears, and two planet gears. The cage is bolted to the crownwheel, and supports the sun gears and planet gears. The two planet gears are free to turn on a single cross-shaft, which is fixed across the middle of the cage. Each of the sun gears is attached to one of the driveshafts, and is also in constant mesh with the two planet gears.

When the car moves in a straight line, the crownwheel transmits the drive through the cage to the cross-shaft. The planet gears are attached to the cross-shaft, so they push the sun gears round, which turn the driveshafts to drive the wheels. In this case, all the differential components rotate as one assembly. When the car turns a corner, the inner wheel slows down and causes the planet gears to turn on their own axis to speed up the outer wheel, but both wheels still receive the same amount of driving power.

A four-wheel-drive car has two differentials, one for the front wheels and another for the rears.

RIGHT A continuously variable transmission (CVT) is far more compact than a conventional automatic transmission, as this unit from a MINI shows

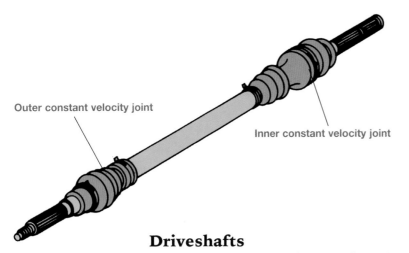

Outer constant velocity joint

Inner constant velocity joint

Transfer box (four-wheel-drive cars

On four-wheel-drive cars, a transfer box is used to divide the drive between the front and rear wheels. Usually, the gearbox output shaft drives the transfer box, which is sometimes bolted straight to the gearbox. The transfer box supplies the drive to the front and rear differentials. On some cars a third differential may be used inside the transfer box, which makes it possible to vary the balance of power between the front and rear wheels.

Driveshafts

The driveshafts transmit drive from the differential to the driven wheels. Each driveshaft is fixed to the differential at one end, and to the wheel hub (on which the wheel is mounted) at the other.

On front-wheel-drive cars, each driveshaft has to be able to move as the suspension moves up and down, and as the wheel turns with the steering. To allow for the suspension and steering movement, constant velocity (CV) joints are fitted to the ends of the driveshafts. The joints are packed with special grease, and are usually covered by flexible rubber covers.

On rear-wheel-drive cars with independent rear suspension, the angle of each driveshaft will change as the rear suspension moves up and down, so universal joints are fitted to the ends of the driveshafts to allow for the movement.

On rear-wheel-drive cars with a solid rear axle assembly, the driveshafts are fitted inside the axle tube. Because the whole axle assembly moves with the suspension, no driveshaft joints are needed.

Propeller shaft

On front-engined, rear-wheel-drive cars, a propeller shaft is used to transmit drive from the gearbox at the front of the car to the differential at the back. On four-wheel-drive cars, depending on the design, a propeller shaft may be used to transmit power from the transfer box to the front and/or rear differentials.

Most propeller shafts have at least one universal joint to allow for suspension movement. Sometimes a bearing is used part way along the shaft to provide extra support.

Propeller shaft

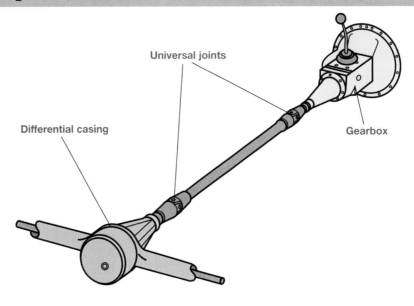

Universal joints

Differential casing

Gearbox

Steering

Steering systems have to be carefully designed to work in conjunction with the suspension. The steering system must allow the driver to keep the car pointing straight ahead, even when driving over bumps, and the driver must be able to steer the car without too much effort.

Steering design

If the front wheels both turned through exactly the same angle when the steering wheel was turned, the tyres would tend to scrub and wear out very quickly. This is because for the car to turn in a circle, the wheel on the inside needs to turn through a larger angle than the wheel on the outside of the turn. The steering and front suspension systems are therefore designed to allow this to happen.

The main components of the steering system are the steering wheel, the steering column, the steering gear and the track rods. The steering column connects the steering wheel to the steering gear. The steering gear (often called a 'steering rack') transforms the rotary movement of the steering wheel into a linear movement to move the car's wheels, and the track rods connect the steering gear to the wheel hubs.

Power steering

Many cars are fitted with power steering, to make it easier for the driver to turn the steering wheel. Some heavy cars with wide, low-profile tyres would be almost impossible to steer at low speeds without power steering. Most power steering systems use hydraulic pressure to increase the effort applied to the steering wheel by the driver, with an engine-driven pump supplying the hydraulic pressure. Some cars use an electric power steering system.

The system has to be carefully designed so that the amount of assistance given is proportional to the effort applied by the driver, and so that the driver can still 'feel' what's happening to the front wheels.

Typical steering layout

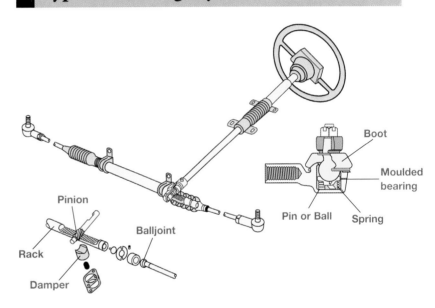

Boot
Moulded bearing
Pin or Ball
Spring
Pinion
Balljoint
Rack
Damper

Typical power steering system layout

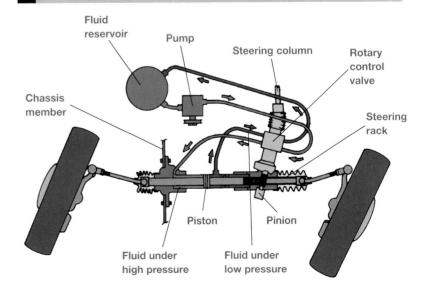

Fluid reservoir
Pump
Steering column
Rotary control valve
Chassis member
Steering rack
Piston
Pinion
Fluid under high pressure
Fluid under low pressure

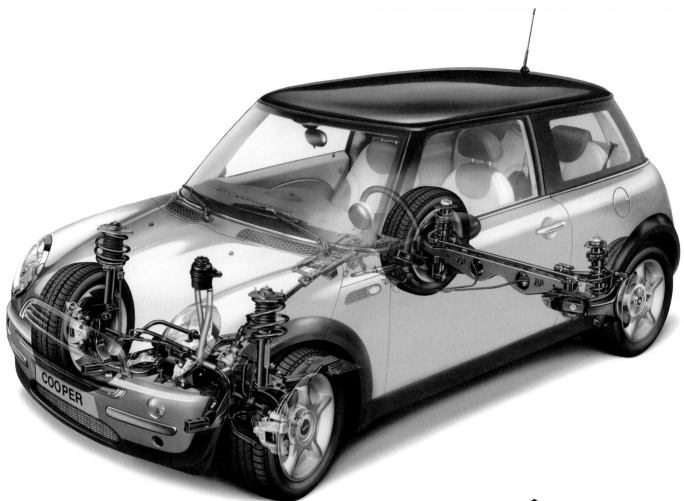

Suspension

The suspension has two jobs – to keep the tyres in contact with the road, enabling the driver to control the car; and to cushion the car's occupants from bumps in the road, providing a comfortable ride.

Suspension design

The design of the suspension is always a compromise, because the characteristics needed to give a comfortable ride generally won't give good handling, and vice versa. For a comfortable ride, a reasonably soft suspension is needed to cushion the car's body from bumps in the road surface. For good handling, a stiff suspension is needed to keep all four tyres in contact with the road, and to keep the car's body as stable as possible.

The suspension on most cars uses a combination of springs and shock absorbers (or 'dampers') to help absorb road shocks and to control the up-and-down movement of the wheels. An anti-roll bar may be used at the front and/or the rear of the car to resist the tendency of the body to 'roll' during cornering. The suspension components are mounted on the body using insulating rubbers to reduce the transmission of shocks, noise and vibration from the suspension to the body.

Suspension systems are very precisely designed, and springs and shock absorbers are carefully chosen to suit the weight and handling characteristics of the particular model of car. Worn or damaged suspension components will affect the handling and braking of the car, and can be very dangerous.

Shock absorbers (or 'dampers')

When one of the car's wheels hits a bump the suspension spring is compressed, and when the bump has passed the spring rebounds back past its rest position and starts to bounce around, or oscillate. This effect might make the car's occupants feel seasick, and will affect the handling. Shock absorbers absorb the energy from the springs, which reduces unwanted oscillations.

Most shock absorbers are designed to be 'double-acting' which means that they resist movement to 'bump' and 'rebound' (up and down motion). Shock absorbers are usually oil or gas-filled.

BELOW A typical front suspension assembly for a front-wheel-drive car. The shock absorbers are integral with the coil spring assemblies – known as a MacPherson strut assembly

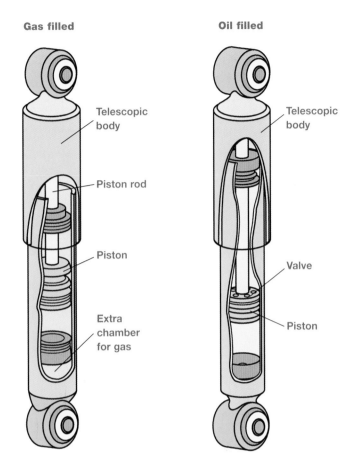

Gas filled — Telescopic body, Piston rod, Piston, Extra chamber for gas

Oil filled — Telescopic body, Valve, Piston

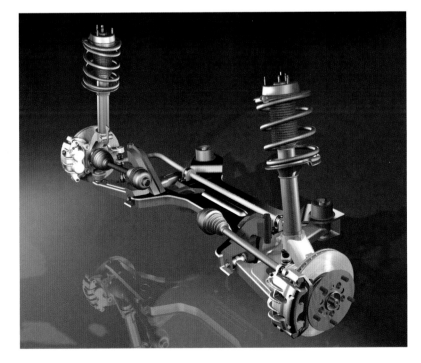

Worn shock absorbers

When shock absorbers wear, it will cause poor handling and braking because the car's body will move more than usual, and the wheels will tend to bounce when they hit bumps. Driving a car with worn shock absorbers can be very dangerous.

To check your car's shock absorbers, press down and then release each corner of the car in turn. The corner of the car should move back up to its original position, and then settle. If the suspension rises up and bounces when you let go, or if you hear a hissing or knocking sound as the suspension moves, the shock absorber is probably worn or faulty.

Many tyre and exhaust specialists offer a shock absorber fitting service at reasonable cost.

Brakes

Early cars had mechanical (cable- or rod-operated) brakes. As braking technology improved hydraulic braking systems were introduced, and all modern cars have hydraulic brakes. The brakes work by forcing friction material against a rotating metal disc or drum. Friction slows the disc or drum, and converts the car's forward energy into heat.

Brake hydraulic systems

The hydraulic system multiplies the pressure the driver applies to the brake pedal, to increase the pressure at each brake.

The brake pedal operates a piston inside a master cylinder full of fluid. When the pedal is pressed, the piston moves, causing fluid to move from the master cylinder along a narrow pipe. The movement of the fluid moves a second piston at the other end of the pipe, which operates the brake. When a car is braking, about two-thirds of its weight acts on the front wheels, so the front brakes normally have bigger pistons than the rear ones, to provide more pressure to the front brakes than the rears.

If there's a leak in the hydraulic system the fluid can escape, so the brakes won't work properly. As a safety measure the hydraulic system is split into two separate circuits, with two pedal-operated pistons in a single master cylinder. Usually, each circuit operates one front brake and the rear brake diagonally opposite, so that if one of the circuits develops a leak the car will still stop in a straight line. Some systems are split front and rear, one circuit operating both front brakes, the other operating both rear brakes. Modern braking systems are efficient and reliable, but they must be maintained properly to ensure safety. The fluid in the braking system deteriorates with age, and it must be renewed at the manufacturer's recommended intervals – usually every 2 years.

Disc brakes

Front disc brakes are used on all modern cars, and disc brakes are also often used at the rear.

A disc brake assembly consists of a caliper and a disc. The caliper incorporates one or more hydraulic cylinders and pistons and carries two brake pads. The caliper straddles the disc, and is mounted on a fixed part of the front suspension. The disc is fixed to the rotating hub that turns with the wheel. When the brakes are applied both brake pads are forced against the disc, slowing it down.

Each brake pad consists of a metal backing plate, with friction material bonded to it. Eventually the friction material will wear away, and the pads will have to be replaced.

Drum brakes

Rear drum brakes are used on many cars, and you may find them fitted to the front of some classic cars.

A drum brake assembly consists of a hydraulic cylinder (or 'wheel cylinder'), two metal brake shoes, a backplate, and a drum. The drum is fixed to the rotating hub that turns with the wheel. The brake shoes fit inside the drum and are curved, with friction material on their outer faces. The shoes are mounted on the backplate, which is mounted on a fixed part of the rear suspension. One end of each shoe rests against an anchor point, which acts as a pivot, and the piston pushes the other end outwards in the hydraulic cylinder when the brake pedal is pressed. When the brakes are applied, the shoes press against the inner surface of the drum, slowing down the drum and wheel. When the brakes are released, return springs stretched between the two shoes pull them away from the drum, allowing the drum and the wheel to turn freely.

Typical brake system

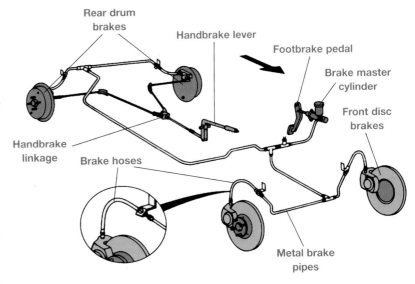

Rear drum brakes

Handbrake lever

Footbrake pedal

Brake master cylinder

Front disc brakes

Handbrake linkage

Brake hoses

Metal brake pipes

Hydraulic cylinder

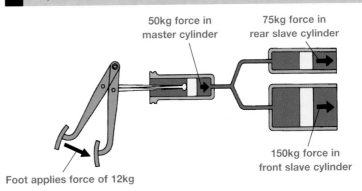

50kg force in master cylinder

75kg force in rear slave cylinder

150kg force in front slave cylinder

Foot applies force of 12kg

Drum brake

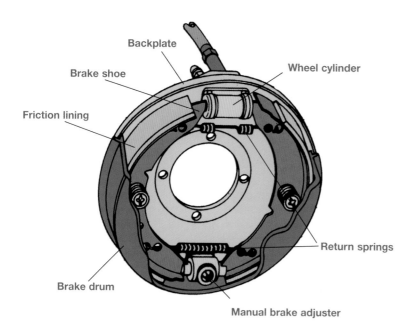

Backplate

Brake shoe

Wheel cylinder

Friction lining

Return springs

Brake drum

Manual brake adjuster

As with brake pads, the friction material on the brake shoes will eventually wear away, and the shoes will have to be replaced, although because less braking effort is applied to the rear wheels rear brake shoes will last much longer than front brake pads.

Servo-assisted brakes

A heavy car needs a lot of pressure on the brake pedal to give maximum braking power. Using a servo reduces the effort the driver has to apply. The servo is usually operated by vacuum from the engine's inlet manifold (on cars with diesel engines a vacuum pump is usually fitted to operate the servo, because on a diesel engine there's no vacuum in the inlet manifold).

A diaphragm inside the servo is connected to a pushrod, which operates the hydraulic master cylinder pistons. When the brake pedal is pressed, air flows into the chamber behind the diaphragm, and because there's a vacuum on the other side the air pushes the diaphragm forwards, operating the brakes. The amount of assistance that the servo gives is proportional to the pressure the driver applies to the brake pedal.

If the servo develops a fault, the brakes will still work, but the driver will need to press the pedal much harder to slow the car down.

Brake servo unit

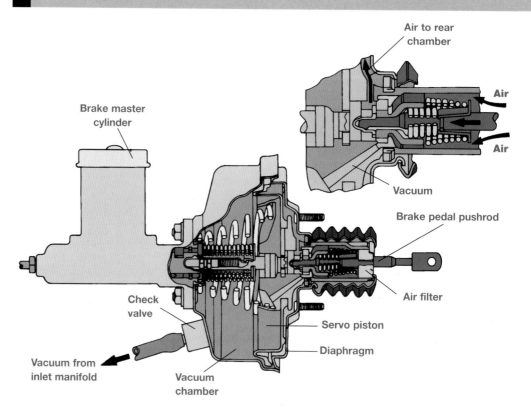

Air to rear chamber

Air

Air

Brake master cylinder

Vacuum

Brake pedal pushrod

Air filter

Check valve

Servo piston

Diaphragm

Vacuum from inlet manifold

Vacuum chamber

Handbrake (or 'parking brake')

The main job of the handbrake, or parking brake (on some cars, such as Mercedes, it's operated by a foot pedal rather than by hand!) is to allow a car to be parked safely without the risk of it rolling away. Usually, it works by applying the rear brakes mechanically, although on some cars – particularly some Citroëns – it operates on the front wheels.

The parking brake operates independently of the brake hydraulic system, and the brakes are usually applied by cables, or sometimes electrically.

ABS (Anti-lock Braking Systems)

Anti-lock braking systems are designed to stop the car's wheels from locking under heavy braking. Some very early systems worked only on the front wheels, but most systems work on all four wheels.

ABS works by detecting when a particular wheel is about to lock. It then reduces the hydraulic pressure applied to that wheel's brake, releasing it just before the wheel locks, and then re-applies it.

The system consists of a hydraulic unit, which contains various solenoid valves and an electric fluid pump, four roadwheel sensors, and an electronic control unit (ECU). The solenoids in the hydraulic unit are controlled by the ECU, which receives signals from the wheel sensors.

If the ECU senses that a wheel is about to lock, it operates the relevant solenoid valve in the hydraulic unit, which isolates that brake from the master cylinder. If the signal from the wheel sensor suggests that the wheel is still about to lock, the ECU switches on the fluid pump in the hydraulic unit and pumps the fluid back from the brake to the master cylinder, releasing the brake. Once the speed of the wheel returns to normal the pump stops and the solenoid valve opens, allowing fluid pressure back to the brake, and so the brake is re-applied. This whole cycle can be repeated many times a second, and this can cause pulses in the hydraulic circuit, which can be felt as rapid vibrations at the brake pedal.

The system relies totally on electrical signals. If an inaccurate signal or a battery problem is detected the ABS is automatically shut down, and a warning light on the instrument panel will come on. Normal braking will always be available whether or not the ABS is working.

ABS can't work miracles – stopping distances will always be greater on slippery surfaces. The greatest benefit of ABS is that it prevents skidding and allows the driver to steer while braking hard.

ABS system

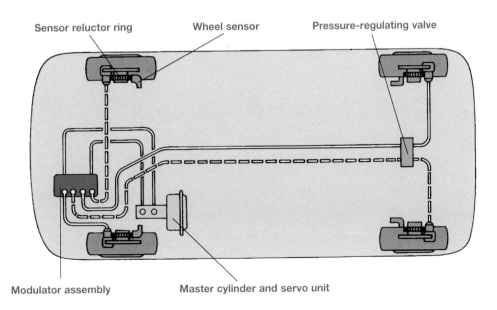

Sensor reluctor ring   Wheel sensor   Pressure-regulating valve

Modulator assembly   Master cylinder and servo unit

Wheels & tyres

The wheels and tyres are essential parts of any car, but are often overlooked. It's worth remembering that the only contact the car has with the road is through its tyres, which transmit 'feedback' to the driver through the wheels and steering. So, the wheels and tyres deserve to be looked after.

Wheels

Most cars have either pressed steel or aluminium alloy wheels. The tyres are fitted directly to the wheels, and a bead on the edge of the tyre seals against the wheel rim to stop air escaping – modern tyres don't use inner tubes.

To avoid vibration inside the car, the wheels and tyres must be balanced accurately so that there's no vibration when they rotate. Whenever a new tyre is fitted to a wheel, the wheel and tyre assembly should be balanced. Wheels and tyres are balanced using a special machine, and if any adjustments are necessary small weights are stuck onto the edges of the wheel rim.

Fitting non-standard wheels

Often, non-standard wheels are fitted, especially aftermarket alloy wheels. These can transform the looks of a car, but it's important to bear in mind that not all wheels fit all cars.

The original-equipment wheels fitted to a car are carefully designed to work with the suspension and steering, and if the wrong sort of replacement wheels and tyres are fitted it can seriously affect the handling – and, in the worst cases, the safety – of the car. Even if second-hand wheels appear to fit, they may have the wrong 'offset' (a measurement of how far the middle of the tyre tread is spaced from the wheel hub), which can affect the car's handling and can cause extra stress on the suspension and steering components.

Always make sure that – unless you're lucky enough to own an exotic sports car with different tyre sizes at front and rear – all four wheels are of the same size, and that they are suitable for use on the particular model of car that you have. Most aftermarket wheels are available in several different versions to suit different makes of car.

Tyres

All tyres are made from rubber, but there are a huge number of different rubber compounds and tread patterns available to suit different types of car and different driving conditions.

Tyres must be kept in good condition, as steering, braking and acceleration forces are all transmitted to the road through them. Worn or damaged tyres can be extremely dangerous, and cause a significant number of road accidents each year.

No matter how well you look after your tyres, they'll wear out eventually. It's difficult to say how long tyres should last, because individual conditions vary so much. What is certain is that neglecting or abusing tyres will definitely shorten their life.

Tyres must be free from damage, correctly inflated, and must have enough tread to give the necessary grip. Check the correct pressures with your car's handbook. Note that pressures should be checked when the tyres are cold (car not driven for at least 30 minutes), and that the pressures may be different for front and rear tyres, and also for fully loaded conditions. The pressure marked on the side of the tyre is the maximum pressure to which the tyre can be safely inflated, not the pressure that the tyres on the car should be pumped up to.

LEFT Tyres are vitally important, as the only contact the car has with the road is through the four small areas of tyre rubber touching the road surface

BELOW When a new tyre is fitted to a wheel, small balance weights may be attached to the wheel rim to balance the wheel/tyre assembly, preventing vibration

RIGHT Tyres should be checked regularly. Here the tread depth is being measured

BELOW Tyres have a big impact on a car's styling, but they also have a significant effect on the way a car handles on the road

Choosing new tyres

When the time comes to fit new tyres to your car, the huge choice available can be baffling. The most important issue is to make sure that you buy the correct size. Any good tyre specialist will be able to advise, and will know which size of tyres to supply by looking at the markings on your existing ones.

It's always worth shopping around to get the best deal – there are plenty of tyre specialists around, and the difference in the prices quoted by different dealers can be surprising.

You may be quoted prices for 'premium' tyres as well as 'mid-price' and 'budget'. Often, the only significant difference between 'premium' and 'mid-price' tyres is the brand name – as a general rule you will pay a premium for a well-known brand. Most of the major tyre manufacturers have a second 'mid-price'

range, sold under a different brand name but offering very good value for money, with no significant reduction in quality. On the whole you get what you pay for with tyres, so although budget tyres are cheaper than those from the big brand names, they often don't perform as well and wear out more quickly.

As tyres are so important, buy the best that you can afford.

Wheel out of balance?

If your car has a wheel out of balance it will usually be felt as a vibration inside the car. Often, the vibration will only be felt at a particular speed, or will suddenly become worse at a certain speed.

A wheel may go out of balance if one of the balance weights falls off (which is quite common) or as the tyre tread wears. It's also common for a wheel to go out of balance if it's suffered damage, for example from hitting a pothole or from 'kerbing'.

As a general rule, a vibration that can be felt through the steering wheel indicates that a front wheel is out of balance, whereas an out-of-balance rear wheel will usually cause a vibration that can be felt through the floor.

Tyre size markings

All tyres carry standard tyre size markings on their sidewalls, such as '185/70 R 13 87T'. These markings indicate the exact specification of the tyre, and the meanings of the various markings in the example cited are as follows:

185   indicates the width of the tyre in mm.

70   indicates the ratio of the tyre section's height to its width, expressed as a percentage. If no number is present at this point the ratio is considered to be 'standard', which is 82 per cent.

R   indicates the tyre is of radial ply construction (older tyres used a 'cross-ply' construction).

13   indicates the wheel diameter for the tyre is 13 inches.

87   is an index number that indicates the maximum load the tyre can carry at its maximum recommended speed.

T   represents the maximum permitted speed for the tyre, which should be equal to or higher than the car's maximum possible speed.

Note that some tyres have the speed rating symbol positioned between the tyre width and the wheel diameter markings, attached to the 'R' radial tyre reference, for example '185/70 HR 13'.

Speed rating symbols for radial tyres

Symbol	kph	mph
P	150	93
Q	160	99
R	170	106
S	180	112
T	190	118
U	200	124
V (after size markings)	Up to 240	Up to 150
H (within size markings)	Up to 210	Up to 130
V (within size markings)	Over 210	Over 130
Z (within size markings)	Over 240	Over 150

On some tyres, you may notice markings at various points around the edge of the tyre, such as 'TWI' or another symbol, with an arrow above pointing to the edge of the tread. These markings show the positions of the 'tread wear indicator' bars that are moulded into the tread on some tyres. The bars run across the tread, and when the tread wears down level with any part of any of the bars the tyre should be renewed, as if the tread has worn down to the indicator bars the tread depth is approaching the legal minimum.

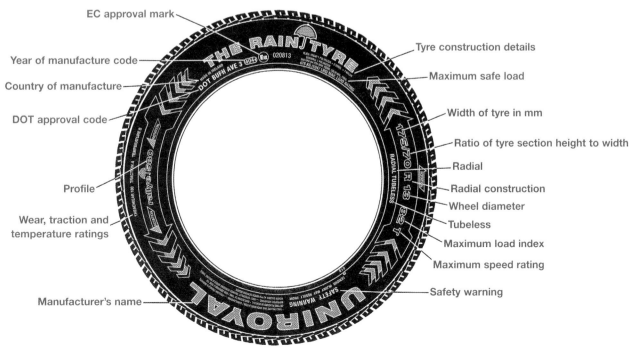

EC approval mark

Year of manufacture code

Country of manufacture

DOT approval code

Profile

Wear, traction and temperature ratings

Manufacturer's name

Tyre construction details

Maximum safe load

Width of tyre in mm

Ratio of tyre section height to width

Radial

Radial construction

Wheel diameter

Tubeless

Maximum load index

Maximum speed rating

Safety warning

Electrical
systems

The electrical system on all modern cars consists of a 12-volt battery, an alternator, a starter motor, and various electrical accessories, components and wiring. Modern systems are all 'negative earth' – this means that the battery negative lead is connected directly to the car's body, which cuts down on the wiring needed and simplifies the layout of the electrical system.

Wiring looms

To simplify a car's wiring, and to make it more reliable, the wiring is normally arranged in 'looms'. The wiring looms are connected together using large multi-plug connectors, and the wires inside each loom are wrapped with cloth tape or plastic sheathing to protect them against chafing and accidental damage. To cut down on costs, often only one or two different types of wiring loom are made for a particular model of car, regardless of the standard equipment and options fitted. This means that sometimes there will be wiring connectors hanging from the loom that aren't used – for example, there may be wiring connectors for front fog lights, but front fog lights may not be fitted to all models – so don't worry if you find a mysterious connector which doesn't seem to be connected to anything!

The battery

The battery's job is to act as an electrical reservoir to supply electricity to operate the car's electrical systems when the engine isn't running, or when the load on the electrical system exceeds the output from the alternator. The battery also has to provide electricity to operate the starter motor when starting the engine.

Most modern cars have a lot of electrical equipment fitted, which means that there's a heavy load on the battery. The standard equipment batteries fitted to cars are almost always 'maintenance-free', which means that they don't need to be topped up with electrolyte, as was the case with older battery types. Most batteries are supplied with a guarantee, and as a rough guide a battery should normally last at least three or four years under normal conditions before needing to be replaced.

The alternator

Once the engine's running, the alternator – which is driven from the engine by a belt – supplies the electricity to operate the various electrical systems (engine management system, lights, electric windows, instruments, etc), and keeps the battery fully charged. The output from the alternator is carefully controlled so that it remains within certain limits whatever the speed of the engine – this prevents damage to the battery and the electrical components.

If the alternator is faulty, the instrument panel 'charge warning' light will usually come on, to indicate that the alternator isn't charging the battery as it should. Although it should be possible to drive on normally with the charge warning light on, it's likely that the battery will eventually run flat, so it's best to stop as soon as convenient to have the problem investigated.

The starter motor

The starter motor is a very powerful electric motor, which turns the engine over until it starts. On most starter motors, when the ignition key is turned to the start position an electrical solenoid moves the starter gear into engagement with a toothed ring fitted to the outside of the engine's flywheel. Power is then supplied to the motor to spin the flywheel until the engine starts. Once the engine has started, a one-way clutch prevents the motor being driven by the engine, until the solenoid is switched off to disengage the starter motor gear from the flywheel.

Fuses and relays

Fuses and relays are vital components of the electrical system. Fuses are used to protect electrical components and circuits against damage from high loads when there's a fault in the circuit. They consist basically of a wire of an exact pre-determined thickness that's designed to melt and break the circuit when the electrical current exceeds a set level – which is what usually happens if there's a short circuit in a wire or component. The main fuses are usually located in a fuse box inside the car, and can be easily replaced.

Relays are used as switches in electrical circuits. If a component needs a high current to operate it, it will need thick wiring to cope with the current. If the high current runs to a switch, the wiring to the switch must be thick enough to carry the current. To avoid having to use a lot of thick wiring throughout the car's wiring looms (which would make the looms bulkier and

heavier), relays are used. A relay is a solenoid that operates one or more sets of electrical contacts. The high current is passed to the contacts, and a low current is used to operate the solenoid. This means that thinner wiring can be used in the circuit from the switch to the relay.

ABOVE An exploded view of the main components of a typical alternator, showing how they fit together to form the complete unit

LEFT A typical starter motor bolted in place on the engine – in this case a Mini engine

BELOW A typical engine compartment fuse/relay box, fitted to a MINI, shown with the cover removed

Accessories and modifications

Fitting accessories to your car enables you to tailor it to your exact needs, and will give it a touch of individuality. There are a vast number of products available, and car accessories are big business.

Where to buy accessories

Most car manufacturers have an accessories catalogue, and many contain everything you could ever possibly need, and possibly a few things that you don't!

Manufacturer's accessories will be designed specifically for your car – for example, tailor-made floor mats should fit perfectly and may incorporate your car's logo. However, this luxury usually comes at a price. You'll find that you can buy good-quality accessories from car accessory shops and motor factors far more cheaply than from an authorised dealer. Accessories sold by a reputable accessory shop are usually of the same standard as the car manufacturer's own products, and may sometimes be the exact same products but with different branding. It's really a matter of personal choice as to where you choose to buy accessories.

Sometimes you can save money by buying second-hand accessories, but you need to be careful. It's a good idea to steer clear of second-hand electrical components, because it's going to be very difficult to tell whether or not they're in good condition, and if they aren't they're likely to be difficult to repair. Beware of buying accessories from market stalls or car boot sales, as there's little chance of getting your money back if they prove to be faulty or incomplete.

Buying the right accessories

If you're thinking of buying any accessory which is likely to be specific to your car (such as roof bars, towing hitches, etc), make sure that you have enough information to hand to ensure that you buy the correct components. You'll normally need to provide the make, model, and the date of registration of your car, and you may need to provide the Vehicle Identification Number or Chassis Number – your car's handbook will show you where to look for these, and they can also be found on the car's V5 Registration Document.

With some accessories, it's probably worth paying to have them professionally fitted. Accessories such as car phones and alarm systems can be complicated to fit, and the work may involve removing interior trim panels and tapping into the vehicle wiring. If you feel confident that you can tackle these sorts of jobs yourself, make sure that you follow the manufacturer's instructions. If you're having an accessory fitted professionally, and the work involves tampering with any part of the car, make sure that it will be covered by a warranty.

ABOVE From walnut veneer/gold-plated tables and in-car entertainment systems...

If you're going to replace any of the car's standard components (such as the steering wheel or roadwheels), make sure that you keep the original components (if they're in good condition); then you can refit them when you sell or trade-in the car. You can then keep the accessories for your next car, or sell them separately.

Warranties

If your car is relatively new you need to be careful that you don't invalidate the warranty by fitting non-approved accessories. This is particularly important with accessories such as alarm systems where fitting involves tampering with the car's wiring, or items such as aftermarket sunroofs, where the body panels have to be drilled and cut (this may invalidate the manufacturer's corrosion warranty).

Insurance

If you're fitting expensive accessories (in-car entertainment, or expensive alloy wheels), make sure that you tell your insurance company – otherwise the accessories might not be covered if they're stolen or damaged.

If you're planning to fit trim parts, such as sporty body kits, or spoilers, bear in mind that this could affect your car insurance premium – you'll normally have to pay an increased premium if the car bodywork has been modified, and if you don't declare the modifications to your insurance company they may not pay up if you have to make a claim!

LEFT ...to alloy wheels – from one end of the accessories spectrum to the other!

Caring for your car

Bodywork

Cleaning your car's bodywork regularly will help to protect it against damage and deterioration, and it's also one of the most vital elements in preserving your car's value when you come to sell it or trade it in. Of course, you'll also have that 'feel-good' factor of driving around in a nice shiny car!

Washing a car

Regular washing is just about the easiest and most important thing you can do to look after the bodywork, but there are several options – you can use the good old bucket, sponge and elbow-grease method, a car-wash, or a jet-wash.

Car-wash

A car-wash is an easy option, and you don't even have to get out of your car, but you can usually spot a car that's regularly been through a car-wash from the light scratches on the paintwork, most often on the wings and roof. Bear in mind that tiny pieces of dirt can easily lodge in car-wash rollers, which then become an instant scouring pad! Car-washes recycle their water, and if the filters aren't regularly cleaned they don't always extract all the dirt. If a car-wash is well-maintained you shouldn't have any of these problems, but it's worth bearing them in mind before joining the queue to put your pride-and-joy through the rollers.

Also bear in mind that many car-washes operate using a 'token' system, and you may have to buy a token from the garage attendant before you can use them. It can be embarrassing to find yourself at the front of the queue with no token!

Jet-wash

A jet-wash is a great option if your car is particularly dirty after driving on a muddy or salty road. Most jet-washes have various different programmes, and you can select the best one to suit your needs. Jet-washes are very good for removing stubborn dirt and mud, and you can blast dirt off from underneath the car as well. Don't wear your best clothes when you're visiting the jet-wash though, as you'll probably get wet, and quite possibly dirty! The only real downside with a jet-wash is that it can be quite expensive to use regularly and, depending on when you want to use it, you may have to join a queue.

As with car-washes, also bear in mind that you may need to buy a token to use a jet-wash.

Bucket and sponge

Washing your car yourself will enable you to concentrate on any particularly dirty or tricky areas. You'll also be able to spot any stone chips or other damage, so that you can take action before they turn into bigger problems as rust starts to take hold.

Here are a few tips to help you get the best results when washing your car:

- Rinse the car first using cold water and a sponge to get rid of dirt and mud, and scrub the wheels. Thick mud can be soaked off using a hose.
- Always use a proper car shampoo, which will usually contain wax. This will thoroughly clean the paintwork, and you'll end up with a nice shiny finish. Don't use household detergents (like washing-up liquid) instead of car shampoo – they're much too harsh, and they can damage the paint. Don't use too much soap, as it will be hard to rinse off and will leave a smeary film.
- Don't wash the car in bright sunlight, because the water will dry almost straight away, giving a blotchy finish. Cold water on very hot paint can cause tiny cracks in the finish. Bright sunlight will also dry out the wax in the shampoo, which can discolour plastic trim, giving a whitish blotchy finish.

- Take care not to put your sponge down on the ground, where it can pick up dirt and grit that could scratch the paint.
- When you've finished with the shampoo, rinse off with plenty of cold water, using a hose if possible. Dry off the bodywork using a soft chamois leather, which will absorb the water and give a shiny finish without streaks.

ABOVE A car-wash is probably the easiest way to clean your car – you don't even need to get out of your seat!

BELOW Essential tools for Sunday morning car-washing duties – a good-quality chamois leather, a sponge and a clean bucket

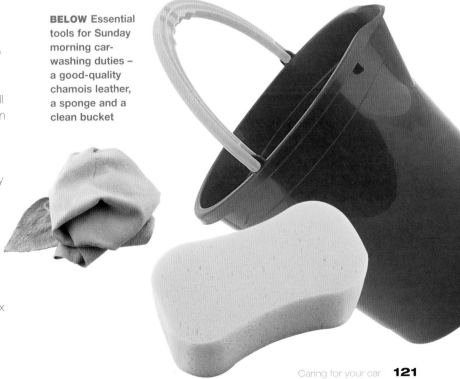

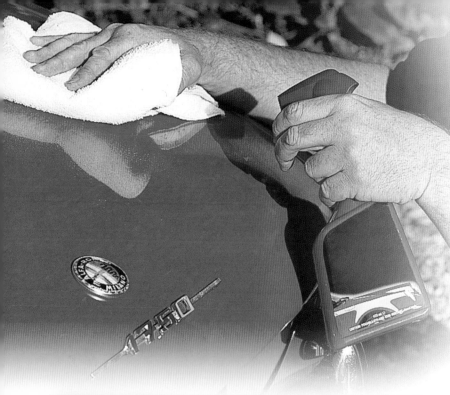

Polishing a car

If you find that the water no longer 'beads' on your car's paintwork when it rains or when you wash it, a coat of polish wouldn't hurt.

Most modern polishes use wax and/or silicone, and these clean the paintwork and leave a layer of protective wax on top. Read the label to make sure that the polish is suitable for your car – for example, some polishes can't be used on metallic paintwork.

Almost all modern paint finishes are made up of two coats – a base colour coat, with a clear coat of resin or lacquer over the top. Don't use abrasive polishes on such finishes, or you'll remove the clear coat.

The following tips will give you the best results when polishing your car:

- Don't polish in strong sunlight. If you do, the polish will dry immediately, and it's likely to be hard to remove – you may even end up scratching the paint trying to get the polish off!
- Before you start polishing, wash the car, and dry it thoroughly.
- You'll need two soft cloths – one for applying the polish, and one for buffing-off. Cotton cloths are best, as they avoid the problem of small particles of cloth sticking to the paint as you polish.
- It's best to work on one panel at a time – if you try to put polish on the whole car in one go before you rub any of it off, the polish you put on first will have dried by the time you come to buff it.
- Apply a thin, even layer of polish using a light circular motion, then let it dry to a haze (not a white powder), and lightly buff it off using your buffing cloth.
- If you get polish on the glass, rub it off with a clean cloth straight away unless the label says it's suitable for glass – most polishes aren't.
- If the polish gets onto plastic trim panels it can discolour them when it dries. You can get rid of these marks using a grease or wax remover (available from most car accessory shops), but read the label to make sure that it's suitable, and follow the instructions. You can restore the look of plastic trim parts using a plastic cleaner or colour restorer (again, read the instructions). These can work wonders with faded plastic, but make sure you wipe any overspill off the paintwork straight away.

Restoring matt paint

If your car is finished with a 'solid colour' paint, which doesn't have a clear coat sprayed over the top, as the car gets older the paintwork might start to fade, looking dull and dirty even after you've washed it.

As long as things haven't got too bad you should be able to revive the paint using a colour restorer. A wide range of paint restoration products is available – some are more abrasive than others, some are especially for metallic paint, and some are coloured for use on a certain paint colour. All these products work by removing a layer of paint, so take care!

Here are a few tips on how to use paint restoration products:

- It's best to start off with a restorer which is only mildly abrasive. Paint is easy to take off, but you can't put it back on! Try it out on a small area first to see what the results will be like before you start on a large panel – don't rub too hard, as some products remove paint very quickly.
- You'll need plenty of soft cloths. Use separate cloths for applying the colour restorer and for buffing-off, changing the cloths as they become covered with paint. Cotton cloths are best, to avoid the problem of bits of cloth sticking to the paint as you work.
- Once you're satisfied with the results, apply a coat of polish to the whole car.

Sometimes a paint finish with a clear coat can deteriorate too, and the clear coat can start to lift off, although this is rare. There's a variation on this problem where air gets between the clear coat and the base paint, oxidising the paint. This appears as a white blotchy layer under the clear coat. Unfortunately, there's no easy fix for either of these problems – the only long-term fix is to have the affected area professionally resprayed.

Touching up paint chips and scratches

If you notice a chip or a scratch when you're cleaning the car, it's best to touch it in as soon as you can, before it starts to rust or fill with dirt and develop into a more serious problem.

Choosing the right touch-up paint

Every car has a paint code, which is usually stamped onto a metal plate when the car is painted at the factory. If you're going to buy paint from a car manufacturer's approved parts department, take your car along – the staff will know where to find the code, often on a plate under the bonnet.

Car accessory shops also sell touch-up paint – all you need to know is the manufacturer's name for the paint colour, and when the car was built. Although aftermarket paints are usually a close match to the original colour, they're rarely exact matches. If you want to be sure of an exact colour match it's wise to buy the paint from an approved dealer parts department.

You can usually buy touch-up paint in two forms – easy-to-use 'touch-up sticks', or spray-cans. The stick consists of a small canister of paint, with a brush built into the lid. Sometimes you'll also get a wire brush for removing rust and flaky paint from the scratch, but take care if you decide to use it – the sharp bristles can make a mess of perfectly good paint.

If your car has a two-coat finish, with a clear top coat, you should be supplied with two paint sticks or spray cans in a kit – one stick or can containing the colour coat, and the other the clear coat.

OPPOSITE Polishing your car will not only keep it looking pristine, but will also protect the paintwork

Using touch-up paint

Firstly, bear in mind that touching up a small chip or scratch (1) using a touch-up stick is a quite straightforward job, but using a spray can is an entirely different proposition, because to spray successfully you need to mask surrounding areas to prevent overspray, and spray inside a well-ventilated garage, or at least away from any wind or draughts. It's also important to keep the spray nozzle clean all the time you're spraying. A detailed procedure for spray-painting isn't included here because it could be a whole book in itself, but here's a guide to touching up using a touch-up stick:

- Use the wire brush supplied with the touch-up stick (2), or a small piece of fine wire wool, to remove any rust from the chip or scratch. Try not to damage the surrounding good paintwork (wrapping wire wool around the end of a pencil helps).
- Next, clean around the affected area. It's best to use plain water – anything else might damage the paintwork, or stop the new paint sticking. Let the paintwork dry fully.
- The paint must be thoroughly mixed, usually by shaking the touch-up stick for a few minutes – follow the instructions. Apply a small amount of paint, using the touch-up stick brush (3) or, better still, a very fine artist's brush. Work slowly, and brush one way. Try to 'fill' the scratch, and don't let the new paint build up higher than the good paint around the scratch. With a two-coat finish, follow the instructions and apply the clear coat after the colour coat has dried properly.
- Wait a few days for the paint to dry completely, then rub the painted area using a polishing compound (or a very mild abrasive colour restorer) to blend in the new paint (4). Once you're happy with the result, wash and polish the car to finish off.

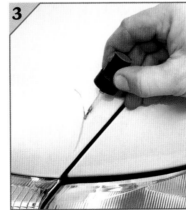

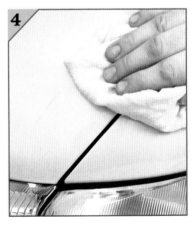

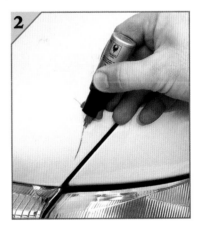

Glass

To keep your car's windows clean, it's best to use a proper car glass cleaner, available from car accessory shops. You can use household glass cleaners, but check that they won't damage the plastic trim or paint. Some household cleaners are very watery, and will run off the glass before you get a chance to use your cloth! To wipe the glass, a soft cotton cloth will usually do a better job than a paper towel. Keep a small sponge or a chamois leather in the car to wipe away condensation and smears.

Wheels

Regular cleaning of the wheels will help to keep them in tip-top condition and will also help you to spot any damage to wheels and tyres. If alloy wheels are neglected they'll soon begin to deteriorate, and a build-up of road grime and brake dust can be difficult to remove and can eventually cause staining. It pays to clean your car's wheels whenever you clean the bodywork.

To clean wheels effectively, it's best to use a stiff-bristled (but not wire!) brush, with plenty of water. Brush the wheels thoroughly to remove the worst of the dirt before sponging. If your car has alloy wheels, using an alloy wheel cleaner and a brush should get rid of most of the dirt. Always follow the instructions on the packaging when using wheel cleaner – some cleaners are caustic, in which case wear gloves and don't get the cleaner on the car's paintwork. Once you've got alloy wheels clean, polishing them will make dirt easier to remove in the future. You can use a special alloy wheel polish, or if your wheels have a clear-coat finish ordinary wax car polish will give good results.

Whilst you're cleaning the wheels, it's a good idea to check them and the tyres for damage and wear. If you notice any problems it's worth seeking a second opinion from a garage or tyre specialist – damaged wheels and worn or damaged tyres are both common causes of accidents.

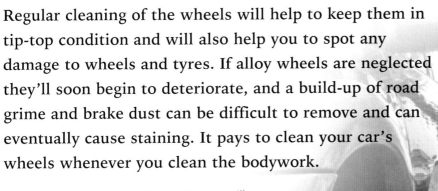

Cleaning the
interior

Keeping your car's interior clean can be a full-time job, especially if you have children or if you carry pets often, but regular cleaning will stop dirt and stains from causing permanent marking.

Fitting floor mats can be a big help – they'll stop the worst of the dirt from marking the carpets, and they can simply be lifted out and brushed or washed off when cleaning the car.

A large range of interior cleaning products is available, including various types of upholstery cleaner, dashboard cleaner, carpet cleaner, etc. It's worth shopping around to buy the products that suit your needs. You don't need a cupboard full of bottles to clean your car, but the right products will certainly help. As well as removing grime, many of these products will help to keep the car smelling fresh.

A good vacuum cleaner will be a big help, along with the right attachments – regular vacuuming will make interior cleaning a lot easier. Don't forget to vacuum the boot and under the seats – it can be surprising, and shocking, just how much dirt gets under the seats!

Inspect the carpets, and if you find any stains use a spray-on cleaner, working it in with a nail-brush and vacuuming or sponging off, according to the instructions. You'll probably find the worst ground-in dirt on the driver's side carpet, especially near the pedals.

Check the seats for marks and use fabric cleaner to deal with these. Allow any dampened seats and carpets to dry before using the car. If you have access to a suitable wet-and-dry vacuum cleaner this can be used to speed up the drying.

Plastic trim cleaner can revive tired or matt trim, and will also protect it against staining and strong sunlight, which can cause fading over time.

Windows are best cleaned using a chamois leather, but difficult marks can be removed with a glass cleaner, buffing finally with a soft cloth. Over time the plastic trim on some modern cars releases vapours into the air, which can cause a greasy film to build up on the interior glass – this is best removed with glass cleaner.

LEFT Suitable plastic cleaner should be used to clean plastic trim parts – spray the cleaner onto a cloth to avoid overspray onto surrounding components

LEFT To avoid trailing a power lead out to your car when vacuuming, you can buy a car vacuum cleaner which can be connected to the cigarette-lighter socket

RIGHT Car vacuum cleaners are inexpensive and usually come with a range of attachments to reach awkward nooks and crannies

FAR LEFT Take out the floor mats and shake them to get rid of loose dirt before vacuuming the carpet

LEFT Use a foam fabric or upholstery cleaner to remove any stubborn marks from the carpets

Weekly checks

Even if you decide not to do your own servicing, there are a few simple weekly checks that can easily be done without special tools. These checks will only take about ten minutes and can help you to spot any problems before they develop into more serious trouble, as well as helping to keep your car in tip-top condition.

Weekly checks checklist

- Engine oil level check
- Coolant level check
- Brake fluid level check
- Power steering fluid level check
- Washer fluid level check
- LHM fluid level check (certain Citroën cars)
- Wiper blade check
- Battery check
- Tyre check

Checking the engine oil

You'll need

1 Park the car on level ground, and make sure the engine has been stopped for at least five minutes, then find the oil level dipstick (check your car's handbook for its location) and pull it completely out of its tube. The top of the dipstick is often brightly coloured to help you find it.

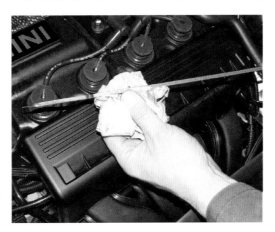

2 Wipe the oil off the dipstick using a clean cloth, and look for the oil level markings on the bottom end of the dipstick.

3 Push the dipstick slowly all the way back into its tube, then pull it out again and check the oil level. The level should be between the upper and lower marks. If the level is near the lower mark, you need to top up.

a clean cloth

a funnel

engine oil of the correct type and grade for your engine

4 To top up, find the oil filler cap on the top of the engine – check your car's handbook for its location, as there may also be filler caps for other systems and you don't want to pour oil into the wrong one!

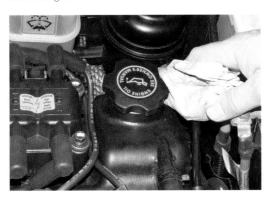

5 Remove the oil filler cap – some caps unscrew and others are a push-fit – and pour in a little oil. A funnel will help to avoid spills.

6 Wait a few seconds for the oil to drain down to the bottom of the engine, then re-check the oil level on the dipstick (repeat steps 1 to 3). If the level is still below the upper mark repeat the topping-up procedure until the level reaches it. Don't overfill the engine with oil, as this can cause leaks and possibly damage.

7 When you've finished, refit the filler cap tightly, wipe away any spills, and make sure that the dipstick is pushed all the way into its tube.

a clean cloth

water

antifreeze

Checking the coolant level

1 Make sure that the engine is cold, and that the car is parked on level ground. If you've driven the car recently, and the engine has reached normal operating temperature, allow it to cool for a couple of hours or so before checking the coolant level.

2 Find the coolant reservoir (check your car's handbook for its location), and check that the coolant level in the reservoir is up to the correct mark, or between the 'MAX' and 'MIN' marks.

3 If the coolant needs topping up, place a wad of rag over the top of the filler cap and slowly unscrew the cap to release the pressure in the system. NEVER unscrew the filler cap if the engine is hot.

4 Top up the level using a 50/50 mixture of clean water and antifreeze to bring the level up to the appropriate mark.

5 When you've finished, refit the cap tightly and wipe away any spillage.

Checking the brake fluid level

a clean cloth

brake fluid

! If you have a Citroën car, refer to 'LHM fluid' section on page before topping up.

1 Make sure that the car is parked on level ground, then find the brake fluid reservoir (check your car's handbook for its location), and check that the brake fluid level in the reservoir is up to the correct mark, or between the 'MAX' and 'MIN' marks.

2 If the fluid needs topping up, slowly unscrew the cap from the reservoir. Many brake fluid reservoir caps have a small float attached to their undersides, which operates the low brake fluid level warning light – if yours has this, allow the fluid to drain from the float back into the reservoir before lifting it out. Place the cap on a wad of clean cloth to catch any drips.

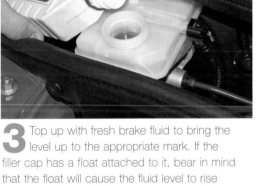

3 Top up with fresh brake fluid to bring the level up to the appropriate mark. If the filler cap has a float attached to it, bear in mind that the float will cause the fluid level to rise when you refit the cap.

4 When you've finished, carefully screw the cap tightly back into position, where applicable making sure that the float slides smoothly back into the reservoir. Wipe up any spillage.

5 Not all cars have a clutch fluid reservoir because not all cars have a hydraulic clutch, and even some of those that do have a sealed hydraulic system where the level can't be checked – check your car's handbook for details of what type of clutch is fitted. To check the clutch fluid level, proceed in exactly the same way as described for the brake fluid level check.

To check power steering fluid level

power steering fluid of
the correct type

1 There are various different types of power steering fluid reservoir, and the method of checking the fluid level varies depending on the type. Refer to your car's handbook for details of the type of reservoir fitted and how to check the fluid level.

2 If you need to remove the reservoir filler cap to check the level, wipe around the cap first, then unscrew it.

3 Read off the fluid level. Some power steering fluid reservoirs have a level dipstick attached to the filler cap, whilst others have a transparent reservoir with markings on the outside, similar to a brake fluid reservoir. Sometimes there may be 'HOT' and 'COLD' level markings for use depending on whether the engine is hot or cold – the level should be up to the appropriate mark.

4 If the fluid needs topping up, wipe around the filler cap and remove it if not already done, then top up to the correct mark. Don't overfill. If the reservoir has a dipstick, wipe the dipstick, then refit the cap/dipstick, unscrew it again and re-check the fluid level.

5 When the level is correct, refit the cap to the reservoir, making sure that it's secure, and wipe up any spillage.

To check the washer fluid level

1 It's a good idea to top up the fluid reservoir every week, unless you can see that it's already full. First of all, check your car's handbook to find out the location of the washer fluid reservoir. Some cars with a rear window washer system have a separate fluid reservoir for the rear window in the boot, but most have a combined reservoir under the bonnet. Similarly, cars with a headlight washer system may have a separate reservoir, usually under the bonnet.

a funnel

water

2 If you need to top up, wipe away any dirt from around the filler neck, then pull off the filler cap.

3 Fill the reservoir with a mixture of washer fluid and clean water (you can pour the two in separately). Some washer fluids are designed to be used undiluted, so check the packaging for details. Use a funnel to avoid spillage.

washer fluid
(NOT antifreeze)

4 Whenever you check the washer fluid level it's a good idea to check that the washer jets are working. To do this, close the bonnet, switch on the ignition and operate the washers. You can clear a blocked washer jet by poking the nozzle gently with a pin. You can also use the pin to swivel the nozzle 'eyeball' so that the jet is correctly aimed – aim the jets so that the washer fluid hits the glass slightly higher up than you want it, because when the car is moving the airflow will tend to push the jet of fluid down.

a clean cloth

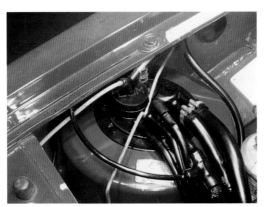

LHM hydraulic fluid

To check the LHM fluid level (certain Citroën cars)

! Certain Citroën cars use a hydraulic system to control the suspension, brakes and power steering. This system uses a special hydraulic fluid (LHM). As with any hydraulic system, a need for frequent topping-up can only be due to a leak, which should be found and fixed without delay. Your car's handbook will tell you which type of hydraulic system your car has.

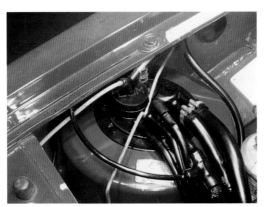

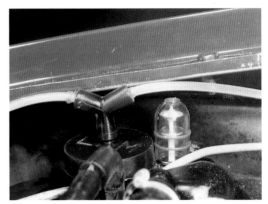

1 Start the engine, and with the engine idling set the suspension height control lever to the 'Maximum' position. The fluid reservoir is located at the side of the engine compartment.

2 The fluid level is indicated by a sight glass on top of the fluid reservoir in the engine compartment. The level indicator float should be between the two rings on the sight glass – the level indication is only accurate when the car has stabilised at its maximum height.

3 If you need to top up, use clean LHM fluid. Remove the filler cap on top of the fluid reservoir, and top up until the level indicator float is between the two rings. When the level is correct, refit the reservoir cap and stop the engine.

WARNING

The fluid used in some Citroën hydraulic systems is LHM mineral fluid, which is green in colour. The use of any other type of fluid, including normal brake fluid, will damage the hydraulic system rubber seals and hoses. Keep the LHM fluid sealed in its original container. Note that most Citroën cars with conventional suspension (springs and shock absorbers instead of hydraulics) use conventional brake hydraulic fluid in the braking system, and automatic transmission fluid in the power steering system – don't use LHM fluid in these systems.

Buying the correct fluid

If you need to top up any of the fluids it's important to make sure that you use the correct type for your car. Using the wrong type is likely to cause problems, and in the worst case damage.

Engine oil

First, check your car's handbook to see what type of oil the manufacturer recommends. Sometimes the recommended oil type is marked on the engine, or on one of the body panels under the bonnet. Often a range of oils is recommended.

The two main things to look out for in the oil specification are the viscosity (thickness) grade shown by the 'SAE' rating, and the quality (indicated by the 'API' or 'ACEA' rating). These specifications will be marked on the oil packaging, and most well-known brands will be suitable – if the packaging doesn't have any specifications marked on it, don't buy it!

Also consider what type of oil you're going to use. The cheaper oils are usually 'mineral-based', the mid-price oils usually 'semi-synthetic', and the expensive oils 'fully-synthetic'. The more expensive, synthetic oils give better protection but are only really needed in very high-performance engines. The mineral-based oils give enough protection for most normal engines, although some manufacturers recommend semi-synthetic oil.

la peau. Protégez l'environnement: L'élimination du produit et de son emballage doit être effec Fiche de donnée de sécurité disponible sur demande pour les professionnels. Pour informati N.V. - S.A., Uitbreidingstraat 60-62, B 2600 Berchem, tel. 03-2866205.

Meets or exceeds the protection and performance standards of most major manufacturers and lubricant industry authorities. SAE 5W-30, API SL/CF, ILSAC GF-3, ACEA A1/B1

OPEN   POUR   CLOSE
Please travel/store upright. Do not store in vehicle once opened   Castrol Limited, Swindon, England.

Coolant

Coolant is usually made up of a mixture of water and antifreeze, although some types of coolant are used undiluted. Check your car's handbook to see which type of coolant it uses. There are actually very few types available, but some manufacturers use 'long-life' coolant which should not be mixed with other types, as it may cause sludge to form in the engine. If your car doesn't use 'long-life' coolant it probably has a glycol-based coolant in the system, and most glycol types can be mixed, but check on the packaging to make sure.

If you need to top up and you're not sure which type of coolant is used in your car, take it to your local dealer, who should be able to advise.

Brake and clutch fluid

Most cars use conventional hydraulic fluid in the brake and clutch systems, but it's important to note that some Citroën cars use a special mineral-based 'LHM' fluid in the hydraulic system, and this must not be mixed with conventional hydraulic fluid – see page 134.

Check in your car handbook to see which type of fluid is recommended. Usually the specification will be for 'DOT 3', 'DOT 4' or 'DOT 5' hydraulic fluid – always make sure that you use the correct type. The 'DOT' specification will usually be marked clearly on the fluid packaging.

Brake fluid should always be stored in a closed, airtight container, as it absorbs water from the atmosphere, which will cause the fluid to deteriorate. Always use clean fluid from a sealed container for topping up purposes.

AP Lockheed DOT 4 Motor Vehicle Brake Fluid exceeds F.M.V.S.S. No. 116 DOT 4 specification and current specification S.A.E. J1703. Typical Dry Boiling Point: 270°C Typical Wet Boiling Point: 173°C

Suitable for all hydraulic Clutch & Brake Systems except for those requiring Mineral Oil and can be mixed with all brake fluids conforming to the above specification. FOLLOW VEHICLE MANUFACTURER'S

Power steering fluid

Various types of power steering fluid are used in cars, and most systems use automatic transmission fluid (of which there are several types). Check your car's handbook for details of the type of fluid to use.

Washer fluid

Any good washer fluid can be used, but don't be tempted to use washing-up liquid or any household cleaners, as they will cause smearing of the glass and could damage the paintwork. NEVER use antifreeze in the washer fluid system, as it will attack the paintwork.

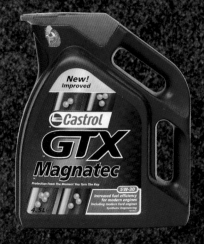

a clean cloth

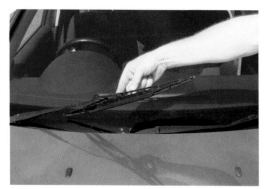  

1 Lift the wiper arm from the glass until it locks in the upright position, taking care not to allow it to spring back against the glass. If the arm doesn't lock in position, hold it firmly whilst you check the blade.

2 Wipe the cleaning edge of the blade using a clean cloth dipped in undiluted washer fluid.

3 Run a finger along the edge of the blade to check the rubber for damage. If there are any cracks or splits a new blade should be fitted.

4 To fit a new blade, first turn the blade at right angles to the arm. Some blades have securing tabs that need to be released before the blade can be removed. Note which way round the blade fits before removing it, to help when fitting the new blade.

5 Depending on the type of new wiper blade you're fitting, fit the correct adaptor to it – check the instructions supplied with the new blade for details.

6 Fit the new blade to the arm, making sure that it's pushed fully home, then lower the arm gently onto the glass. Check that the wipers work before driving the car.

Buying wiper blades

If you're on a tight budget you can buy wiper blade 'refills', which means just the rubber, but to fit these you'll need to dismantle the blade and this can be very fiddly. It's advisable to renew the whole blade because the springs that hold the blade against the glass weaken with age.

You can buy new wiper blades from most car accessory shops, and from authorised car dealership parts departments. When you go to buy new blades you'll need to know the make, model, and the year of manufacture of your car.

To check the battery

! A quick battery check each week can help to avoid trouble – faulty battery connections and flat batteries are among the most common causes of breakdowns.

1 Check the outside of the battery for damage, and check that the cable clamps are tight to ensure good connections – you shouldn't be able to move them. Also check the battery cables for cracks and fraying.

2 If the cable clamps are corroded (white fluffy deposits), clean them with a small wire brush. Corrosion can be prevented by spraying the terminals with battery terminal protector, available from car accessory shops. Alternatively, you can smear the terminals with petroleum jelly.

3 Most modern batteries are maintenance-free and don't need to be topped up. Maintenance-free batteries usually have a condition indicator fitted, which often consists of a disc that changes colour to indicate the condition of the battery. Usually a green disc indicates that the battery is OK, and the disc darkens as the battery condition deteriorates. Check your car's handbook or the battery instructions for details of how to use the indicator.

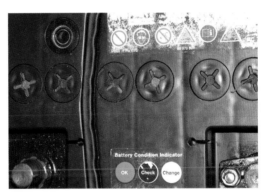

a small wire brush

Buying a new battery

If you need to buy a new battery, where do you start? It's worth phoning around for a few quotes, but make sure you're comparing like with like. The cheapest battery is not necessarily the best buy.

Your car's handbook should tell you what 'capacity' battery it needs. This is measured in several ways, but the most commonly used figure is the amp-hour (Ah) rating. Generally, the bigger the engine, the higher the battery capacity needs to be. Most car accessory shops should be able to help you, but you'll need to know the make, exact model and engine size of your car.

There are three basic types of car battery – 'conventional', 'low-maintenance' and 'maintenance-free' (most modern cars have maintenance-free types) – and it's best to buy a similar replacement.

Conventional batteries need to be checked at regular intervals. This involves checking that the electrolyte fluid level is correct, and you may need to top up the battery with distilled water. Plugs are provided in the top for checking and topping-up.

A low-maintenance battery is similar to a conventional battery, but requires less frequent checking.

Maintenance-free batteries require no maintenance. They're designed to last for a number of years, and are often fitted with a condition indicator which will show when the battery needs to be recharged or replaced – check the battery instructions for details.

Most new batteries come with a guarantee. As a guide, the guarantee will usually be for one or two years for a conventional battery, and four years or more for a maintenance-free battery. Be wary of batteries with no guarantee. Read the guarantee conditions carefully, and keep the receipt and guarantee card safe.

a tyre pressure gauge

a tyre tread depth gauge

a tyre pump

1 Working on each wheel in turn, unscrew the tyre valve dust cap and put it somewhere safe. If any dust caps are missing, replace them.

2 Check the tyre pressure by pushing the nozzle of the gauge firmly onto the valve so that no air can be heard escaping. Check the reading on the gauge against the pressures recommended in your car's handbook. Note that the pressures for front and rear tyres are often different, and if you're carrying a heavy load the pressures should usually be increased. Also note that the pressures should usually be checked cold, which means that the car should not have been driven recently. Bear in mind that on a hot summer's day there can be a significant difference in the pressure reading for a tyre on the side of the car in the shade compared to that on the side in direct sunlight – tyre pressures increase with temperature.

3 If the pressure needs increasing slightly, you can either drive to the nearest garage or else use your pump according to the instructions.

4 Check the pressure again. If it's now too high, remove the gauge and gently press the pin in the centre of the tyre valve to release a small quantity of air at a time. Re-check the pressure with the gauge. Refit the dust cap when you've finished.

5 Don't forget the spare tyre – it's a good idea to inflate this to the highest of the pressures suggested for your car.

6 All tyres must have at least the minimum legal amount of tread – that's 1.6 mm in the UK, although in practice it's better to change tyres well before they become this worn. Most tyres have tread wear indicator bars (see the 'Wheels and tyres' section in Chapter 4), or you can use a tyre tread depth gauge (available from car accessory shops) to check the depth.

7 Carry out a quick check on the condition of each tyre. Look for damage, bulges, or foreign bodies in treads or sidewalls, and for uneven tread wear. If you find any problems it's a good idea to visit a tyre specialist for advice – fit the spare wheel before driving the car if a tyre is very worn or obviously damaged.

Slow punctures

If a tyre needs frequent pumping up, it may be due to a slow puncture.

Check that the valve dust cap isn't missing, and if it is buy a new one and fit it as soon as possible.

If the valve cap is in place and the tyre is losing air it could be due to a leaking valve. If the valve has a serious leak you'll be able to hear a hissing sound. If you can't hear any sound, put a little soapy water around the edge of the valve – over time a leak will tend to produce air bubbles. Even if none of these checks shows up a problem the valve could still be faulty, but the leak may be so slow that you can't detect it.

Another cause of trouble is poor sealing between the tyre and the wheel. This is quite a common problem on cars with alloy wheels if the wheels are old or if the finish is beginning to corrode. The coating on the wheel can flake off, which breaks the airtight seal between the wheel and tyre. Have the wheel and tyre checked by a tyre specialist if you think that this may be the cause of a problem.

Often a sharp object such as a nail or a thorn can stick into the tyre tread without causing an instant puncture. Air may leak out gradually over time. The only solution here is to have the tyre repaired or to fit a new tyre

Service schedules

For a car to be reliable it must be properly maintained. It doesn't matter what make or type of car you have, eventually things will wear out because the components aren't designed to last forever. Maintenance isn't going to prevent every possible failure or breakage, but it will help to prevent common failures and it will minimise the risk of your car letting you down. Don't forget that regular servicing will also help to preserve the value of your car when you come to trade it in or sell it.

Every car manufacturer specifies a service schedule for each of its models, and it's important to make sure that this schedule is followed. If servicing is neglected, or worse still ignored, it's almost inevitable that sooner or later your car will suffer the consequences, which could prove inconvenient, expensive, or both!

If you have the service record book that was originally supplied with your car when it was new, this will usually contain a service schedule. Often, the service schedule is also given in the car's handbook, but if you don't have a service schedule an authorised dealer for your make of car should be able to provide one.

Whether you have the servicing carried out by a garage, or whether you decide to do it yourself, is a matter of personal choice. DIY servicing will certainly save you money, but you may not have the experience, confidence, or enthusiasm to carry out all the servicing yourself.

Every 12 months or every 20,000 miles (30,000km) – whichever comes first

- Check indicators and lights.
- Check windscreen and headlamp wash/wipe system.
- Renew engine oil and filter.
- Check coolant level.
- Check brake fluid level.
- Check power steering fluid level.
- Check automatic transmission fluid level.
- Check auxiliary drivebelts.
- Check clutch pedal adjustment.
- Renew fuel filter – petrol engines.
- Check handbrake adjustment.
- Check suspension components.
- Check brake pipes and hoses.
- Check fuel lines.
- Check exhaust system.
- Check front and rear brake components.
- Check transmission for leaks.
- Check air conditioning compressor for leaks.
- Check steering rubber gaiters.
- Check track rod ends and driveshaft gaiters.
- Check wheel bolt torque and tyre pressures.
- Check headlight alignment.
- Lubricate door hinges, door stops, locks, bonnet release and tailgate hinges.
- Test drive the car.

Every 12 months, regardless of mileage

- Drain water from fuel filter – diesel engines.
- Check body and underbody for damage (for anti-perforation warranty).

Every 20,000 miles (30,000km), regardless of time interval

- Renew fuel filter.

Every 2 years, regardless of mileage

- Replace batteries in central-locking remote control.
- Renew brake fluid.

Every 2 years or 20,000 miles (30,000km) – whichever comes first

- Renew pollen filter.

Every 4 years or 40,000 miles (60,000km) – whichever comes first

- Renew air cleaner element.
- Renew spark plugs.
- Renew automatic transmission fluid.
- Remove brake drum and check and clean brake shoe components.

Every 8 years or 80,000 miles (120,000km) – whichever comes first

- Replace timing belt and pulleys (it's advisable to replace these components more frequently for many models).

BELOW A typical car manufacturer's service schedule, showing all the recommended tasks to be carried out when servicing

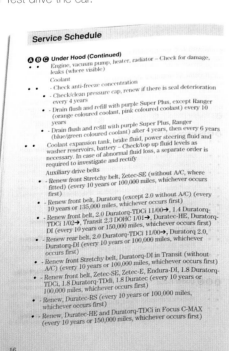

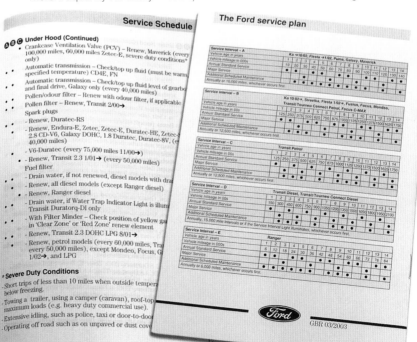

Garage
servicing

If you're going to have your car serviced by a garage, the following advice will help you to make sure that the garage is reputable, that the bill will be reasonable, and that the work is carried out properly.

Choosing a garage

If you need to have work done on your car, whether it's servicing, repair work, or fitting extras, how do you decide where to take it? You may decide to carry out the work yourself, you may have a suitably qualified friend who's willing to help, or you may decide to find a garage to do the work for you.

If your car is still under warranty, always take it to an authorised dealer for your make of car to have any work or checks carried out – if you take it anywhere else you may invalidate the warranty.

If you want to ensure that your car has an authentic service history when you come to sell it, you may decide to have all work done by an authorised dealer. Generally this will be the most expensive option, but you'll have the satisfaction of knowing that the manufacturer's procedures and parts will be used for all the work.

If your car needs tyres, exhaust parts, shock absorbers, or even a new clutch, it's worth trying one of the specialist fitting centres. Many will offer you an all-inclusive price for a particular job, often with a comprehensive warranty, for far less than a garage would charge.

If you're not prepared to pay the rates charged by an authorised dealer, you may decide to take your car to one of the smaller independent garages. Some specialise in a particular make of car and, although they may not be authorised dealers, you'll often find that their expertise is equal to, or even better than, that of the manufacturer's trained personnel. If you're going to take your car to an independent garage it's always worth visiting several in your area, and asking them for a price for the work to be carried out.

At a smaller garage you can't always expect the 'fancy' service provided by a larger dealer – there may not be a carpeted waiting area, and you may not be provided with a courtesy car, but remember that a dealer is building these 'perks' into your bill.

Ask around to see if anyone you know has had good or bad experience of dealing with any of the garages you're thinking of using. Reputation is very important, and it's often better to pay a little extra to take your car to a garage with a known good reputation.

Pricing

When asking for a price for work to be carried out, always ask for a written firm price, and check to see what's included. Most authorised dealers have fixed price 'menu' servicing costs, so you know exactly what you'll be paying for a particular service or job.

The items on a garage bill usually fall into one of three categories: parts, labour, and consumables. Parts include any new parts that may be required during the work. Labour covers the cost of the time taken (in hours) by the mechanic to carry out the work. Consumables covers items such oil, coolant, cleaning fluids, etc. Always ask for an itemised list so that you can see exactly what's been included.

Here are a few things that you should ask when getting a price for a job:

- What's the hourly labour rate?
- How long should the work take?
- Will genuine or pattern parts be used?

- Is VAT included?
- Will the work be covered by a warranty? (Ask for details of the warranty)

If you're comparing several quotes, make sure that you're making a fair comparison, as the prices may be structured differently. You should find that the prices are similar, and by comparing them you'll be able to spot any discrepancies or suspicious costs. If there's anything you don't understand, ask.

You can check the cost of genuine parts by asking at an authorised dealer, and you can compare these prices with those of pattern parts from a motor factor. There will always be a mark-up on parts prices, as a garage will almost certainly pay a 'trade' price for parts that will always be less than the retail price.

Once you decide to have the work done, ask the garage to contact you immediately if they encounter any problems which will involve additional work. If you don't do this, many will carry out the work anyway and charge you accordingly.

If you're having new parts fitted, check whether the work will be covered by a parts and labour warranty; if not, ask why.

BELOW If your car is still under warranty, always take it to an authorised dealer for servicing, otherwise you may invalidate the warranty

Understanding the mechanic

When you're discussing any work to be carried out on your car, don't let the service manager or mechanic baffle you. Always ask if you have any questions. The Glossary at the end of this book should help you to understand the terminology used, and the explanations given in Chapter 4 of how systems work should be useful too. Make sure that you understand what work the garage is intending to do.

Sometimes a garage may point out other potential problems whilst carrying out work on your car. For example, it might be suggested that the brake components are worn, and that you'll need new ones soon. Always check this for yourself, or ask the mechanic to show you the problem. If in doubt, ask for a second opinion from an experienced friend or another garage.

BELOW Most garages will be happy for a mechanic to answer any questions that you might have – never be afraid to ask if there's anything you're unsure about

Checking the work

If components have been renewed, many garages leave the old components in a box in the boot so that you can see that the work has been carried out, and that it was necessary. It's a good idea to ask the mechanic to do this when you take your car in for work to be done.

If your car has been serviced, check that a new (clean) oil filter has been fitted, and pull out the dipstick to check for fresh oil. Often you can spot the areas where work has been carried out, because the areas surrounding the work will be cleaner than the rest of the car.

If the work involved disturbing any gaskets or seals, park the car overnight with a sheet of card or paper underneath (or pick a clean piece of road or driveway) so that you can check for signs of leaks in the morning. If you notice any leaks, take the car back to have them fixed, and don't let the garage charge you for fixing the problem (unless it's totally unrelated to the work they've done).

If the work involved removing the wheels, it's a good idea to check that the nuts or bolts aren't too tight, so that you can remove the wheel if you have a puncture.

Checking the bill

Always ask for an itemised bill, which will give you a full breakdown of all the costs, and will allow you to see exactly what work has been carried out. Here are a few tips for checking that the bill is correct:

- Check the details of the bill against the firm price that you were given, and query any discrepancies. If you find that 'miscellaneous' costs appear on your bill, ask what they are.
- Check the labour costs against the garage's quoted hourly rate, and check that the price of any parts used seems reasonable.
- Check that the work described on the bill has been carried out, and if there's any evidence that you've been billed for work which hasn't been done query it with the mechanic concerned.
- Once you've checked the bill, and you're happy that it's accurate, it's time to dip into your pocket!

Warranties

When you have work carried out on your car, the work should be covered by a warranty. If you have any work done that involves the fitting of new components (especially major items such as an engine or gearbox), make sure that the work and components are covered by a 'parts and labour' warranty. This will cover you against the use of any faulty parts, and any mistakes made by the mechanic that might cause trouble later. Check that the bill states the work is covered by a warranty, and be sure that the warranty period is specified.

DIY Servicing

DIY servicing can save you a lot of money, even if you decide not to carry out all the necessary jobs yourself. Modern cars need far less servicing than older models, and the intervals between services are far longer than they were a few years ago. Even so, garage labour rates can be high, and carrying out your own servicing can save you a lot of money.

Because the steps involved in a specific service procedure vary so much from car to car information for each and every servicing task isn't included in this book. General instructions are provided for some simple renewal procedures that aren't particularly difficult or dirty, but it's important to realise that these are only a few of the jobs that need to be carried out as part of the service schedule. If you're keen to learn more about how your car works and how to service it, then you might find it useful to attend a vehicle maintenance course, such as those run by some adult education centres. You'll find all the information you need for servicing procedures specific to your car in the relevant Haynes *Service and Repair Manual*.

Buying parts

To be sure of obtaining the correct parts, you'll need to know the model and year of manufacture of your car, and it will sometimes be necessary to quote the Vehicle Identification Number (VIN). Your car's handbook will usually show you where to find the VIN. It can also be useful to take the old parts along for identification.

Authorised dealers

This is the best source for parts that are specific to your car – badges, interior trim, etc. It's the only place you should buy parts if your car is still under warranty. You'll generally pay more for parts at an authorised dealer, but at least you can be pretty sure that the parts are the correct ones.

Accessory shops

These are good for servicing components. Filters and spark plugs, etc, bought from a good car accessory shop are usually of the same standard as those used by the car manufacturer. Most of these shops also sell tools and general accessories. Some have parts counters where components needed for almost any servicing or repair job can be bought or ordered.

Motor factors

Good factors will stock all the more important components that are likely to need replacing, as well as servicing components. Prices are likely to be competitive, as most motor factors also sell components to the garage trade.

Other sources of parts

Beware of parts or materials bought from market stalls, car boot sales, etc. These items aren't necessarily sub-standard, but there's little chance of compensation if they are unsatisfactory. It really isn't worth the risk of buying safety-critical components such as brake pads from one of these sources.

Second-hand components obtained from a car breaker or from on-line auctions can be a good buy in some circumstances, but this sort of purchase is best made with the help of someone experienced.

Safety

If you're going to carry out any work on your car, the first priority must always be safety. Never take any unnecessary risks, and always try to use the correct tools for the job you're doing – don't try to improvise.

It's a sensible precaution to wear disposable gloves whenever you're working on a car, as this will protect your hands and will also make it a lot easier to clean them afterwards.

Bear in mind that if you're working under the bonnet and the engine has run recently, various engine components, particularly the exhaust system, can be hot enough to cause serious burns.

If you're working under the bonnet with the engine running, keep well clear of the moving components.

Be careful where you put tools when you're not using them – they can easily slip into inaccessible locations, and on some cars it's very easy to accidentally short-out the battery terminals with metal tools, which can cause damage and possibly a fire.

Tools

A selection of basic tools is essential if you're thinking of maintaining your car. The tool kit supplied with most cars won't allow you to do much more than change a wheel! You don't need to buy the most expensive tools, but generally you get what you pay for, and a good quality set of tools will last for many years.

If you're planning to carry out servicing and maintenance yourself there are a few extra tools you'll need in addition to those recommended in Chapter 3. Here are a few suggestions as to what you might need for basic servicing jobs on most cars (note that you won't need all these tools to carry out the simple servicing jobs described in this chapter):

Do's and don'ts of working on a car

DO

 Wear gloves, or use barrier cream to protect your skin.

 Wear eye protection.

 Keep clothing, etc, well clear of moving parts.

 Remove jewellery and watches before starting work.

 Mop up any spills immediately.

DON'T

 Rush to finish a job, or take shortcuts.

 Use poorly fitting tools that might slip.

 Leave tools or fluids lying around.

ABOVE A selection of good-quality tools is essential if you're intending to carry out DIY servicing. Buy the best tools you can afford

- Comprehensive socket set (with socket sizes from 8mm to 26mm).
- Oil filter removal tool.
- Oil sump drain plug tool (a socket is all that's needed on some cars).
- Oilcan.
- Funnel.
- Oil draining container.
- Tyre pump.
- Tyre pressure gauge.
- Small wire brush.
- Overalls.
- Old newspapers and clean rags for cleaning and mopping up.
- Self-locking grips.
- Brake bleed nipple spanner.
- Brake bleeding kit.
- Soft-faced mallet.
- Ball pein hammer.
- Torque wrench.
- Fine emery cloth.
- Light, with extension lead.
- Hydraulic jack.
- Axle stands.

If you decide to carry out more advanced maintenance jobs you'll need some additional tools, and you can add to your tool kit as you progress.

Once you've built up a reasonable kit you need to keep the tools in good condition. Never leave tools lying around after they've been used. Take care when using them, and don't try to use them for a job they're not designed for.

There are safety standards for tools, and usually the packaging – or the tools themselves – will show that they meet a particular standard. You can buy plenty of tools that don't meet any standards, but they're more likely to let you down and unlikely to last as long. You don't have to buy the most expensive tools, but it's a good idea to steer clear of the very cheap ones. Nevertheless, you'll have to make sensible compromises when choosing. If you're on a limited budget it's best to spend a little more on the tools you're likely to use most often – for instance, a good set of spanners should last you a lifetime, whereas a poor quality set will tend to wear and won't fit properly.

Servicing procedures

The guide to the mileage intervals for each check outlined on page 141 is only a guide, and you should always follow the manufacturer's recommendations. Modern cars require far less servicing than those built a few years ago, partly due to improvements in the reliability of the components and partly due to improvements in lubricants and fluids. The general trend is for servicing intervals to be longer than they were in the past. Sometimes the manufacturer may recommend that the checks are carried out at longer intervals than suggested here, and sometimes at shorter intervals. Bear in mind that some fluids and filters deteriorate with age, so you should always carry out the checks or changes at the recommended time intervals even if you cover very few miles.

Engine oil and filter

In the past, many manufacturers recommended that the oil was changed every 6,000 miles (10,000km), but now it's not uncommon for recommended oil change intervals to be as infrequent as every 20,000 miles (30,000km). In spite of this, it's a good idea – and it certainly won't do any harm – to change the oil more frequently than the manufacturer recommends. Bear in mind that oil deteriorates with age, so you should always change it once a year even if you do very few miles.

To change the oil you'll need plenty of clean cloth, disposable gloves, a draining container (usually about five litres capacity), an oil filter removal tool, a spanner or drain plug key to fit the oil drain plug, a new oil filter, a new oil drain plug sealing washer, a pack of engine oil of the correct type, and a funnel.

Before you start, the car should be parked on level ground and the engine should be warm (after a short run). If you're unsure of the location of the oil filler cap, sump drain plug or oil filter, check your car's handbook, which will normally give details.

You'll need

an oil filter

an oil filter removal tool

a spanner or socket to fit the drain plug

a draining container

a new drain plug seal

a funnel

a clean cloth

engine oil of the correct type and grade

To renew the oil

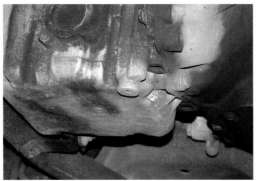

1 Remove the oil filler cap from the top of the engine. Find the oil drain plug in the sump underneath the engine. The oil will come out with some force at first, so position the draining container under the plug so the oil doesn't miss it! On come cars you may have to remove a plastic shield from under the engine compartment for access to the drain plug.

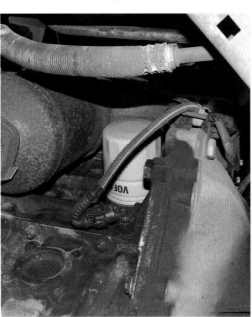

2 Put on the gloves, and slacken the drain plug using the spanner or drain plug key. Unscrew it by hand the last couple of turns, keeping the plug pressed into its hole. When the plug comes out, pull it away quickly so that the oil runs straight into the container.

3 Allow about ten minutes for the oil to drain. Wipe the drain plug clean, then remove the old sealing washer and fit the new one.

4 When the oil stops draining, wipe around the drain plug hole, then screw in the plug and tighten it. Make sure that the plug is tight, but not too tight.

5 Now you need to find the oil filter, usually a cylindrical metal canister near the bottom of the engine at the back, front, or side. Check your car's handbook for details.

6 Reposition the draining container underneath the oil filter, then use the oil filter removal tool to slacken the filter (turn it anti-clockwise). Once the filter is loose, unscrew it by hand. Drain the oil from inside the filter into the container. When you remove the filter from the engine, the oil will probably run down the side of the engine, so be prepared – it's a good idea to place some old rags or newspaper under the engine to catch any spills.

7 Wipe clean around the filter mounting on the engine, using a clean cloth. Take the new oil filter and, using your finger, smear a little clean engine oil on the rubber sealing ring.

8 Screw the new filter onto the engine by hand until the sealing ring touches the engine, then tighten it by hand about another half- to three-quarters of a turn. Pull the draining container and tools out from under the car.

9 Check you car's handbook to see how much oil the engine needs, then pour in about two-thirds of the recommended quantity through the filler hole at the top of the engine. Use a funnel to stop spills.

10 Wait a few minutes for the oil to drain down into the engine, then pull out the dipstick and check the oil level (see the section on 'Weekly checks').

11 Keep topping up the oil and re-checking the level until the level reaches the upper mark on the dipstick. Then refit the filler cap and check that the dipstick is pushed firmly in.

12 Start the engine. The red oil pressure warning light on the instrument panel may take a few seconds to go out – if it doesn't go out, stop the engine! Run the engine for a few minutes and check for leaks around the oil filter and drain plug. Re-tighten slightly if necessary, but don't overtighten.

13 Stop the engine and wait a few minutes for the oil to run down into the engine again, then re-check the oil level. Top up if necessary, but don't overfill. Pour the old oil into a container and take it to your local oil recycling centre. Most waste disposal sites and most garages have a waste-oil tank, and will probably take the oil for you if you ask. Don't pour it down a drain or into the ground!

Air filter

Most manufacturers recommend that the air filter is changed around every two years or 20,000 miles (30,000km).

The filter stops dirt, dust and insects from being sucked into the engine through the inlet manifold. If the element is very dirty or blocked, the engine won't run properly and the fuel consumption might be higher than normal. If the filter is missing or split, dirt may be sucked into the engine, causing expensive damage.

When buying a new air filter you'll need to know the model, engine size and year of manufacture of your car.

Air filters are usually housed in a rectangular plastic casing next to the engine, or a round casing on top of the engine – check your car's handbook if you're not sure of the filter's location. Sometimes you may have to unclip or disconnect a hose or disconnect a wiring plug before you can remove the air filter cover.

You'll need

a new air filter

a clean cloth

To renew the air filter

1 Release the clips and/or unscrew the securing screws, then lift the cover from the air filter housing.

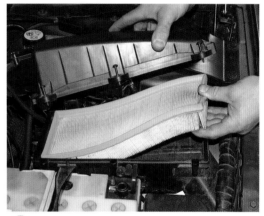

2 Lift out the air filter, noting which way up it's fitted (some filters fit either way up). Make sure that the new filter is the same as the one you've taken out.

3 Wipe out the casing and the cover using a clean cloth. Be careful not to get any dirt or dust into the air intake.

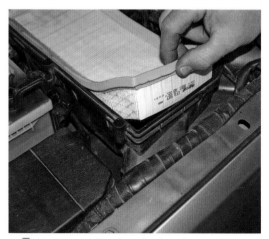

4 Fit the new filter into the housing, making sure that it's the right way up, then refit the cover and secure it with the clips and/or screws.

5 If you had to disconnect any hoses or wiring plugs to remove the filter, don't forget to reconnect them when you've finished.

Automatic transmission fluid

As a rough guide, if your car has an automatic transmission the fluid level should be checked around every 12 months or 6,000 miles (10,000km).

If the automatic transmission fluid level gets low the transmission may not work properly – low fluid level is a common source of problems with automatic transmissions. If the level drops too far it could even damage the transmission. There are several different types of automatic transmission fluid and it's essential that you use the right one, so you'll need to check your car's handbook, or with an authorised dealer. If frequent topping-up is needed have the cause found and fixed without delay.

The following advice is only a guide – you need to check your car's handbook to see exactly how to check the automatic transmission fluid level, but the technique is similar for most cars, using a level dipstick which fits inside a tube attached to the transmission. The level is usually checked with the transmission warm, after a short drive.

To check the automatic transmission fluid level

You'll need

1 With the engine running and the handbrake on, press the brake pedal and move the gear selector lever through all the gear positions, starting and ending in 'P'. Let the engine idle for one minute, then, with the engine still running, pull out the dipstick. Wipe the dipstick with a clean cloth and push it carefully back into its tube.

2 Pull the dipstick out again and check the fluid level. Often you'll find the dipstick has two sets of markings, one for checking the fluid hot (or at high temperature, eg 80°C), and one for checking cold (or at low temperature, eg, 20°C).

3 Read off the fluid level, and if topping-up is needed stop the engine.

4 Usually, topping-up is done through the dipstick tube, so you'll need a bottle with a tube, or a clean funnel, to stop spills. Don't overfill, and be very careful not to allow dust or dirt into the transmission.

5 Start the engine and re-check the level. Stop the engine and top up again if necessary, and finally refit the dipstick when the level is correct.

a clean cloth

suitable automatic transmission fluid

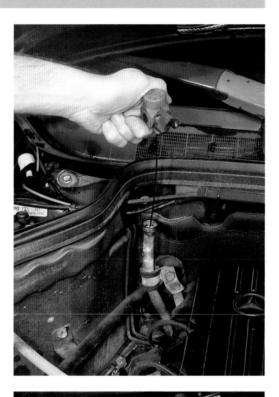

Fuel filter water draining (diesel engines)

WARNING: Diesel fuel is irritating to the skin, so wear disposable gloves when you're doing this job.

Water should be drained from the fuel filter assembly at least every 6,000 miles or six months, or as soon as the 'water in fuel' warning light (if fitted) comes on. It should also be drained at the beginning of winter in order to avoid problems caused by the water freezing.

The fuel filter stops any dirt in the fuel from getting into the fuel injection system. The dirt could otherwise cause blockages, which would make the engine run poorly, or not at all, and possibly cause expensive damage.

As well as filtering out dirt, most fuel filter assemblies incorporate a water separator to prevent any water in the fuel from getting into the fuel system components. The water can be drained off from the filter using a drain plug. The following procedure is only intended as a guide, and you should consult your car's handbook for details of the location of the fuel filter and the exact procedure for your car.

To drain off water

1 A drain plug is usually provided at the bottom of the fuel filter housing. The plug often has a tube fitted to it to help draining.

2 Place a suitable container under the drain plug or tube, then slacken the drain plug and allow fuel and water to drain until water-free fuel emerges. Close the drain plug, then dispose of the drained water and fuel safely.

Auxiliary drivebelts

Auxiliary drivebelts are usually driven from the engine crankshaft pulley and drive engine ancillaries such as the alternator, power steering pump, air conditioning compressor and, on some cars, the coolant pump. One drivebelt may drive all the ancillaries, or several separate drivebelts may be used. As a rough guide, the auxiliary drivebelt(s) should be checked every six months or 6,000 miles (10,000km).

It can be tricky to reach auxiliary drivebelts, and on some cars access may be easier from under the car.

To check a belt

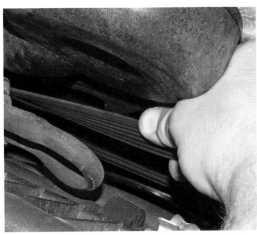

1 Check the whole length of the belt – to do this you might need to turn the engine using a spanner on the bolt or nut fitted to the end of the crankshaft.

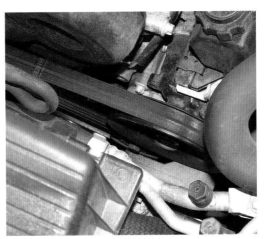

2 Look for cracks, splitting, or fraying on the surface of the belt, and check for signs of shiny patches.

3 If you find any damage or wear a new belt should be fitted.

Pollen filter

Many modern cars have pollen filters to filter the air flowing into the heating/ventilation system. The filter will stop pollen and dust from the atmosphere being drawn into the car's interior.

Most manufacturers recommend that the pollen filter is changed around every two years or 20,000 miles (30,000km). In order to renew the filter you'll probably need to refer to your car's handbook to find out where it's located and how to gain access. Pollen filters are usually located under the scuttle panel at the back of the engine compartment, or behind the facia inside the car, and you might need to remove surrounding trim panels to gain access.

Bulbs
and fuses

A faulty light can be dangerous, and if one of your car's lights isn't working you can be stopped by the police. It's therefore a good idea to carry a set of spare bulbs in your car's tool kit. That way you'll always have suitable spares if you notice that a bulb has blown when you're driving.

Fuses protect a car's electrical circuits from overloads. If an electrical component or system stops working, it could be that the fuse has blown.

Bulbs

Various different types of light bulbs are fitted to cars, and your car's handbook will usually provide a guide to fitting them, and will also tell you which types of bulb you need.

Here's a general guide to fitting a new halogen-type headlight bulb. You may find differences – for instance access, and bulb type – for your car. Before you start, make sure that the headlights are switched off. Remember that a bulb that has just failed or been switched off may be extremely hot.

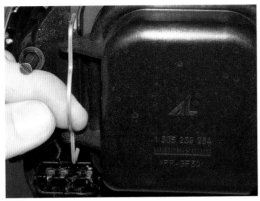

a spare bulb kit

1 Where necessary, unclip the cover from the rear of the headlight for access to the bulb.

2 Disconnect the wiring plug and, where applicable pull the rubber cover from the back of the bulb.

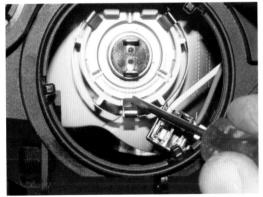

3 Release the spring clip that holds the bulb in place (squeeze the ends of the clip together and pull it away from the bulb-holder), then pull out the bulb.

4 Don't touch the glass on the new bulb with your fingers – hold it with a tissue or clean cloth. If you accidentally touch the bulb, clean it with a little methylated spirit. This is because the moisture in your skin can etch into the glass of a halogen bulb and cause it to fail.

5 Halogen bulbs usually have locating lugs around their edge so that they only fit in one position. Slide the new bulb into position, then secure it with the spring clip. Refit the rubber cover, reconnect the wiring plug and refit the bulb cover, as applicable.

Fuses

Most of the fuses are usually housed in a fuse box, often under the dashboard – your car's handbook will tell you where to find it. A blown fuse can be recognised by the melted wire in the middle.

Never use a piece of wire or any other metal in place of a fuse – not even temporarily. You will almost certainly cause damage, and in the worst case a fire.

Blown fuse

OK fuse

To change a fuse

1 Simply pull the fuse from the fuse box. On some cars you'll find a plastic tool for removing the fuses.

2 The new fuse must be of the same rating as the old one. It should be the same colour, or have the same number (5, 10, 15, 20, 25, 30, etc) stamped on it.

3 Push the new fuse firmly into its slot in the fuse box making sure that the contacts on the fuse slide into the terminals in the fuse box.

4 Switch on the appropriate circuit – if the new fuse blows there's a problem, and you should find the cause of the problem or seek advice before fitting another one.

Fixing a faulty light

If you find that a light isn't working properly and the bulb hasn't blown, the most likely cause is a bad electrical connection.

Corrosion
First of all, check the wiring connectors for corrosion, and also check the contacts inside the bulb-holder. Even if water hasn't got in, condensation can often cause trouble. If you find any corrosion, clean the affected area with abrasive paper or a small wire brush, then spray the components with water dispersant (such as WD-40). In the worst cases you might have to replace the affected parts.

Earth connections
If there's no trace of corrosion, check the earth connections for the light. Usually there's an earth wire running from the light unit to a bolt on a nearby body panel, or plugged into an earth connector block attached to the body. Check that the earth connections to the body are not corroded, and that they're tight. If a connection is bolted to a body panel, unscrew the bolt and try cleaning the area around the bolt with abrasive paper or a small wire brush. Reconnect the earth wire and tighten the bolt, then spray the components with water dispersant.

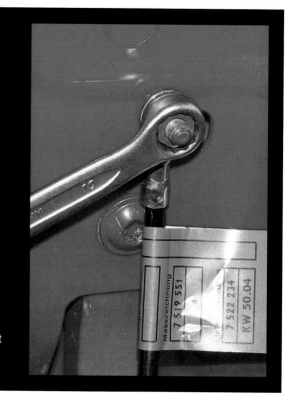

Preparing for winter

Winter puts extra strain on a car, and any minor problems that have been lurking are likely to make themselves known and may cause trouble once winter arrives. Before the onset of winter, it's a good idea to carry out the following checks.

☑ Check the coolant mixture

If the coolant (antifreeze and water) freezes it could wreck your engine. A garage can check the coolant for you, or you can buy a simple and inexpensive coolant tester – follow the instructions supplied with the tester to check the coolant mixture. Refer to the 'DIY servicing' section in this chapter for details of how to check the coolant level.

☑ Check the battery

Battery failure is the most common source of trouble in winter. Check that the battery is in good condition, then clean the battery lead connections and make sure they're tight. If the battery shows signs that it might be getting towards the end of its life, fit a new one before winter starts – refer to 'Buying a new battery' on page 137 for more advice.

☑ Check the wipers and washers

You'll use the wipers and washers a lot in winter. Make sure that the wiper blades are in good condition. New ones aren't expensive, so it's well worth renewing them at the start of every winter. Check the windscreen washer system and the rear window washer system too if you have one.

Always keep the washer fluid topped up, and make sure the washer jets aren't blocked and that they spray onto the screen, not over the top of the roof or onto the bonnet! Refer to the 'Weekly checks' section in this chapter for details of how to check wipers and washers.

☑ Check the cooling system hoses

Look for signs of damage or leaks, and have any problem hoses renewed.

☑ Check the auxiliary drivebelt(s)

Look for damage, and check the tension of the belt(s) – refer to the 'DIY servicing' section in this chapter for details.

☑ Check all fluids and filters

Top up or renew the fluids as necessary, as described in the 'Weekly checks' section in this chapter.

☑ Check all the lights and indicators

Make sure that they work properly, and replace any blown bulbs.

Preparing for an MoT test

In the UK, all cars over three years old must have an annual MoT test. It's an offence to use a car on the road without a valid test certificate (except when driving to and from an MoT test). You'll also have to produce the MoT certificate when buying a tax disc for your car.

Not all garages can carry out MoT tests, but the ones that do usually advertise the service and often display an official sign outside showing that they're authorised to do so.

You're entitled to watch the test being carried out if you wish to, and if you're interested enough to do this you may pick up some useful information about the general condition of your car. A friendly tester may point out to you items that, although not part of the test, may require attention soon.

The MoT test is now carried out 'on-line', and the results of each test are held on a central database.

You won't be able to examine the car to the same standard as a professional MoT tester, and you won't be able to carry out all the checks that feature in the test, as special equipment is required for some of them, but working through the following checks may help you to spot possible problems and get them fixed before taking the car for a test.

Even if you don't want to carry out any checks before the MoT, at least clean the car thoroughly inside and out and, if you can, give the underside a wash too. The tester can refuse to examine a car that's really filthy underneath.

The following checks can be easily carried out without jacking the car up, and without specialist knowledge, but you'll need the help of an assistant for some of them.

Checks carried out from the driver's seat

Handbrake
- Check that the handbrake works correctly. If you have to pull the lever up a long way (too many clicks) the cables probably need adjustment.
- Check that the handbrake can't be released by tapping the lever sideways.
- Check that the lever mountings are secure.

Footbrake
- Check that the brake pedal is secure and in good condition.
- Check for signs of brake fluid leaks on the pedal, floor and carpets.
- Press the brake pedal down and check that it doesn't move down as far as the floor. Release the pedal, then wait a few seconds and push it again. If the pedal moves nearly to the floor before firm resistance is felt, brake adjustment or repair is necessary. If the pedal feels 'spongy' this probably means that there's air in the hydraulic system which must be removed by bleeding.
- Check the brake servo unit by pushing the brake pedal several times, then keeping it pushed down and starting the engine. As the engine starts the pedal should move down slightly – if it doesn't, the servo may be faulty.

Steering wheel and column
- Check the steering wheel for damage.
- Check that the steering wheel is not loose on the column, and that there's no abnormal movement that would indicate wear in the column or its joints.

Windscreen, mirrors and sun visor
- The windscreen must be free from cracks and other damage within the driver's field of vision. (Small stone chips will not cause an MoT failure.)

- All rear-view mirrors must be secure, undamaged and capable of being adjusted.
- The driver's sun visor must be capable of being stored in the 'up' position.

Doors
- Both front doors must be able to be opened and closed from the outside and inside, with the car at rest, and must latch securely when closed.

Seat belts and seats
- Check the webbing of all the seat belts (including the rear seat belts, if fitted) for cuts, serious fraying or deterioration. Fasten and unfasten the belts to check the buckles, and check the retracting mechanism.
- Pull on the belts and buckles to check the security of the mountings.
- The front seats must be securely attached, and the backrests must lock securely in the upright position.

Electrical system
- Switch on the ignition, and check that the horn works.
- Check that the windscreen wipers and washers work.
- On cars fitted with an ABS system, the warning light must illuminate in accordance with the manufacturer's design. Usually, the ABS warning light should illuminate when the ignition is switched on, and (if the system is working correctly) should go out after a few seconds.
- On cars fitted with an airbag system, check the warning light as described previously for the ABS warning light.

Checks carried out from outside the car

Vehicle identification
- The number plates must be in good condition, securely fitted, and easily readable, with letters and numbers correctly spaced.
- The vehicle identification number (VIN) plate under the bonnet must be secure and readable.

Electrical equipment
- Check the operation of all the lights, including the brake lights (you'll need an assistant) and number plate light(s), and check that the lenses and reflectors are clean and undamaged.
- Check the condition of the wiper blades, and renew damaged or perished blades.

Braking system
- Working under the bonnet, check all the brake components, brake pipes and servo unit for leaks, loose mountings, corrosion or other damage.
- The fluid reservoir must be secure and the fluid level correct.

Exhaust system
- Start the engine. With your assistant holding a cloth over the exhaust tailpipe, check the entire system for leaks. You'll be able to hear if the system is leaking. If there are no leaks, the engine will stall if the cloth is held over the end of the exhaust for a few seconds.

Steering and suspension
- Check the shock absorbers as described under 'Worn shock absorbers' in Chapter 4 (see page 105).
- If your car has power steering, check that the pump is secure and free from leaks, and check the power steering fluid reservoir, hoses and pipes for leaks.
- Make sure that the steering lock isn't engaged, then turn the steering wheel slightly from side to side, up to the point where the roadwheels just begin to move. Make sure that there's no excessive free play between the steering wheel and the roadwheels, which would indicate worn steering components.

If your car fails the MoT test
If your car fails its MoT test, this means that it doesn't meet the legal requirements for it to be driven on the road. You must have any problems fixed as soon as possible, and then the car must be re-tested. Your local MoT testing station will be able to give you more details of the regulations for repairing and re-testing your car.

ABOVE An exhaust gas emissions check is an important part of the MoT test, but it isn't possible to check the emissions on a DIY basis

APPENDIX A
Troubleshooting

Modern cars are much more reliable than those of a few years ago, so hopefully you shouldn't need to call on the advice contained in this appendix very often.

Why did it stop?

If the engine stops running suddenly as if the ignition has been switched off it's probably due to an ignition system fault, whereas if the engine splutters or misfires before finally stopping it's usually a fuel system fault. The following chart will give you a few clues.

Symptom	Possible cause
Engine suddenly stops as if switched off	Faulty ignition switch (or switch accidentally turned off!)
	Loose or broken connection or wire in ignition system
	Faulty ignition system component(s)
	Loose or broken battery earth connection
Engine splutters or misfires, loses power and stops	Fuel tank empty!
	Fuel cut-off switch activated (see 'What to do if your car won't start')
	Dirt or water in fuel lines
	Faulty fuel system component(s)
	Water on ignition system components (in bad weather or after going through a flood)
	Faulty ignition system component(s)
Engine makes unpleasant noises and stops	Mechanical failure (such as broken timing belt)

Why won't it start?

If the engine won't start, work through the following flow chart to try to find a clue to the cause – you may not be able to fix the problem yourself, but at least you'll be able to give a mechanic a few clues about the cause of the problem.

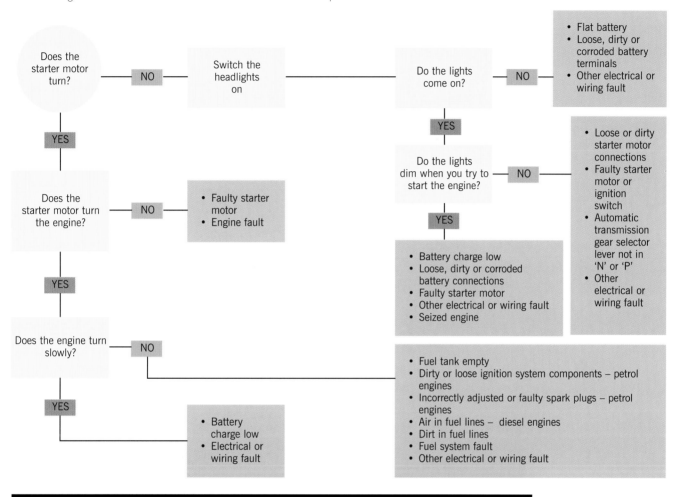

Does the starter motor turn? — **NO** → Switch the headlights on → Do the lights come on? — **NO** →
- Flat battery
- Loose, dirty or corroded battery terminals
- Other electrical or wiring fault

Does the starter motor turn? — **YES** ↓

Does the starter motor turn the engine? — **NO** →
- Faulty starter motor
- Engine fault

Do the lights come on? — **YES** ↓

Do the lights dim when you try to start the engine? — **NO** →
- Loose or dirty starter motor connections
- Faulty starter motor or ignition switch
- Automatic transmission gear selector lever not in 'N' or 'P'
- Other electrical or wiring fault

Does the starter motor turn the engine? — **YES** ↓

Do the lights dim when you try to start the engine? — **YES** ↓
- Battery charge low
- Loose, dirty or corroded battery connections
- Faulty starter motor
- Other electrical or wiring fault
- Seized engine

Does the engine turn slowly? — **NO** →
- Fuel tank empty
- Dirty or loose ignition system components – petrol engines
- Incorrectly adjusted or faulty spark plugs – petrol engines
- Air in fuel lines – diesel engines
- Dirt in fuel lines
- Fuel system fault
- Other electrical or wiring fault

Does the engine turn slowly? — **YES** ↓
- Battery charge low
- Electrical or wiring fault

What to do if your car won't start

There aren't many things more frustrating than an engine that won't start – but try to think logically. Before calling for help, run through the following checks, just in case you can fix the problem yourself.

1 Immobiliser – check that you know how this works, and make sure that you know the starting procedure, otherwise it may seem like you have a 'dead' engine.

2 Automatic transmission – the engine won't start unless the selector lever is in the 'N' or 'P' position. This is a safety feature, and is not a fault.

3 If there's no familiar starter motor sound (or just a clicking noise), then the starter motor may be faulty, or the battery may be flat.

4 You could be out of fuel (faulty gauges have been known, so don't rely totally on the reading). Consider whether this is a possibility (if you haven't just filled up!).

5 On some petrol engine cars there's a cut-off switch that stops the fuel flow in the event of an accident. Sometimes this switch can be triggered by a pothole or a minor bump – you'll have to reset it manually. Check your car's handbook for details, and try resetting it. Most switches can be reset by pushing a button on the top of the switch.

What's that noise?

A strange noise could spell trouble, or it could just be an annoying distraction
– so how do you tell? Here's a guide to help you to identify noises and
decide what to do about them.

Noises from the exhaust

Noise	Possible cause	Remarks
Light 'puffing' or blowing noise when accelerating or decelerating, or when engine is idling	Small hole or crack in exhaust system	Repair temporarily with exhaust putty. Go to exhaust specialist for advice.
Sudden increase in noise, especially when accelerating and decelerating	Hole or crack in exhaust system, or failed silencer exhaust specialist for advice.	Repair temporarily with exhaust bandage. Go to
Metallic rattling or thumping over bumps, or when accelerating and decelerating	Loose or broken exhaust mounting	Repair temporarily with wire. Go to exhaust specialist for advice.

Noises from the brakes

Noise	Possible cause	Remarks
Light squeaking when applying brakes gently for the first time of the day	Normal characteristic of disc brakes	Could be normal.
Squealing whenever brakes are applied	Could be first sign of excessively worn brake friction material	Ask your garage to check – possibly cured by applying special brake grease to the metal brake component surfaces. Renew brake pads or shoes if required.
Deep metallic scraping when brakes are applied, or when the brakes aren't in use	Excessively worn brake components. Trapped stone or dirt between brake disc and pad	Have your garage investigate without delay before further damage occurs.
Chattering or tapping when brakes are applied	Contaminated brake friction material	Damaged brake discs or drums. Have your garage investigate without delay.

Noises from the suspension

Noise	Possible cause	Remarks
Clunks or rattles when driving over bumps	Worn or damaged suspension or steering components. Loose or broken exhaust mounting	Probably not urgent, but have your garage investigate before too long.
Rumbling, growling or clicking noises when turning corners	Worn wheel bearing(s) Worn driveshaft joint (front-wheel-drive cars)	Probably not urgent, but may cause further damage if neglected.
'Hissing' noise when driving slowly over bumps	Badly worn shock absorbers	Drive carefully until new shock absorbers have been fitted – handling and ride may be poor.
Constant clicking noise	Stone embedded in tyre Wheel fouling brake or suspension component	Take the stone out with your penknife! If it's not a stone, seek advice.

Noises from the engine compartment

Noise	Possible cause	Remarks
Squealing	Loose or worn auxiliary drivebelt or timing belt	Probably not urgent, but get it fixed before it breaks.
Continuous hum or whine	Auxiliary drivebelt or timing belt too tight Alternator, coolant pump or power steering pump worn	Probably not urgent, but get it fixed before it gets worse.
Rhythmic slapping when the engine is cold	'Piston slap'	Not a problem as long as it stops when engine warms up.
Light tapping from the top of the engine	Valve clearances incorrect (too large)	Not urgent, but have them adjusted at the next service.
Rhythmic metallic thumping or thudding	Worn engine bearings or camshaft	May be a serious problem. Have it investigated without delay.
High-pitched metallic rattle when engine is under load (accelerating or driving uphill)	Engine "pinking" or "pre-ignition" (poor quality fuel or wrong fuel type, or ignition system fault)	Drive gently until you can fill up with good fuel or have the ignition system checked.

Noises from the transmission

Noise	Possible cause	Remarks
Whine or howl from manual transmission in neutral, quietens or disappears when clutch pedal is depressed	Worn transmission bearing	You can still drive, but have it fixed before it gets much worse.
Whine or howl from manual transmission when clutch pedal is depressed, quietens or disappears when pedal is released	Worn clutch release bearing	You can still drive, but have it fixed before it gets much worse.
Squealing from manual transmission as clutch is engaged or released	Incorrectly adjusted clutch Worn clutch	If adjustment doesn't cure the problem, have it fixed before it gets worse.
Whine or howl from automatic transmission in neutral	Low transmission fluid level Worn or damaged transmission	Check the fluid level. If that's OK, have the transmission checked without delay.
Howl or whine when accelerating or decelerating	Low transmission oil/fluid level Worn bearing in transmission Worn or damaged differential	Check the oil level. If that's OK, you can probably carry on driving for a while, but have the transmission checked before something breaks.
"Graunching" sound from manual transmission when changing gear	Incorrectly adjusted clutch Worn synchromesh units in transmission Badly worn gear teeth	If clutch adjustment doesn't cure it, you probably need a new transmission.

Leaks

A leak may show up as a stain under your car, or you may be forever topping-up one of the fluids. So how do you tell if a leak is serious, or something you can live with for a while?

Here's a quick guide on how to identify possible leaks, and whether or not it's safe to drive the car if you find a leak.

Petrol

Petrol has a strong and distinctive smell, so a leak should be obvious. If you've just filled up with petrol on a hot day, and the car's standing in the sun, the petrol may expand, and liquid or vapour may leak out through the fuel tank breather. Petrol can also leak if you park a car with a full tank on a steep slope. Petrol will evaporate very quickly, so you're unlikely to find a stain under the car.

If the leak isn't due to either of the above causes, have it investigated straight away. Don't drive the car until the leak's been fixed.

Diesel fuel

Diesel fuel has a distinctive oily smell (like domestic heating oil), and is a clear, oily substance. As with petrol, a recently filled tank may leak a little due to expansion. Any other leak is cause for concern. Don't drive the car until the leak's been fixed.

Engine oil

■ Engine oil is usually black, unless it's recently been changed. Clean oil is usually clear or green. Compare the leak with the oil on the end of the oil level dipstick. The most common sources of leaks are the oil drain plug, the oil filter, and the sump gasket under the engine.
■ You can drive with a minor oil leak, but keep an eye on the oil level.

Coolant

■ Coolant usually contains a bright-coloured dye, and has a strong, sickly sweet smell. Old coolant may be rusty or dirty brown, and there may be a white crystalline deposit around the leak. Leaks usually come from a hose, the radiator, or the heater inside the car (you'll smell coolant when you switch the heater on).
■ You can drive with a minor leak, but if you lose too much coolant, the engine could overheat.

Water

■ If a leak looks like clear water, and your car has air conditioning, it may not be a leak but condensation from the air conditioning system. A lot of condensation can be produced on a hot day, which may look like a major leak.
■ See also the sections on 'Coolant' and 'Washer fluid'.

Brake/clutch fluid

■ Brake/clutch hydraulic fluid is clear, thin and almost watery. Old hydraulic fluid gradually darkens. Compare the leak with the contents of the brake or clutch fluid reservoir. Brake fluid leaks usually come from the brake master cylinder or the reservoir in the engine compartment, but may also appear around the wheels or the brake line connections under the car. Clutch fluid leaks usually come from hydraulic line connections, or from failed seals in the hydraulic components.
■ Don't drive the car if you think there might be a brake fluid leak. It's OK to drive with a minor clutch fluid leak, but if you lose all the fluid the clutch won't work.

Manual transmission or final drive oil

■ The oil is usually a tan colour or reddish-pink, although old oil may darken. Transmission oil is thicker than engine oil, and often has a very sickly smell, especially when hot.
■ You can drive with a minor leak, but if the oil level gets too low it can cause serious transmission damage.

Automatic transmission fluid

■ The fluid may be clear or a reddish-brown colour. Compare the leak with the fluid on the end of the transmission fluid level dipstick. Leaks usually come from the transmission casing, or from fluid lines running to the fluid cooler (this could be mounted on the transmission, or incorporated in the radiator).
■ You can drive with a minor leak, but keep an eye on the fluid level.

Power steering fluid

■ The fluid is usually clear or reddish-brown. Compare the leak with the contents of the power steering fluid reservoir. Leaks usually come from fluid line connections, the power steering pump, or the steering gear.
■ You can drive with a minor leak, but keep an eye on the fluid level.

Shock absorber fluid

■ Usually shows up as a dark stain on the shock absorber body.
■ You can drive the car, but you may have a poor ride and poor handling – take care!

Grease

■ Grease is usually black or grey, thick, and very sticky! You may find it under the car if it's leaked from the driveshaft rubber gaiters or steering gear gaiters.
■ You can drive the car, but if much grease has been lost the driveshaft or steering gear could be damaged through lack of lubrication.

Washer fluid

■ Washer fluid usually contains a coloured dye, and has a strong smell of detergent, alcohol or ammonia. The leak could be due to a poor pipe connection, or a leaky washer pump seal in the fluid reservoir.

Engine overheating

Overheating is a serious problem, and can be caused by a number of things. If you're driving on a hot day in summer your car will overheat much more easily in traffic than on a cold winter's day, but provided it's been properly maintained you shouldn't really have any problems.

When the engine gets hot, the cooling fan should cut in to lower the temperature. Normally you'll be able to see this on the temperature gauge – the temperature will go up until the cooling fan cuts in, then the temperature will fall. The cycle might repeat several times until you start moving forwards fast enough for the airflow to cool the radiator without needing the fan.

If the temperature gauge stays in the red, don't be tempted to carry on driving – stop as soon as possible. (As an emergency measure, turning the heater blower onto full speed and selecting maximum heat will bring the temperature down a little, at the cost of discomfort to the occupants!)

What causes overheating? Here are the most common causes:

■ Low coolant level.
■ Faulty cooling fan.
■ Coolant leakage.
■ Faulty coolant pump.
■ Broken coolant pump drivebelt (where applicable).

What to do if your engine overheats

Cars most often overheat when stuck in traffic, so keep an eye on the temperature gauge.

■ If you notice the temperature gauge needle creeping towards the red, or if a temperature warning light comes on – try moving the heater control to 'hot' straight away, and switch the heater blower motor to maximum – this will get rid of some of the heat from the engine. If the temperature doesn't drop, or keeps going up, pull over in a safe place and stop the engine.

■ If you notice steam coming from under the bonnet – pull over and stop as soon as possible. Don't open the bonnet until the steam stops.

■ If no steam is coming from under the bonnet – open the bonnet to help the heat escape, and wait for the engine to cool down. A very hot engine takes time to cool, and you'll have to wait at least half-an-hour before the temperature drops to normal.

■ Check under the car for coolant leakage – coolant is usually brightly coloured (often green, yellow or pink), and will probably be steaming if it's hot. If there's a leak, call for assistance.

■ When the engine has cooled, if there's no obvious sign of leakage – check the coolant level – if there's been no leakage, and no steam, the level will probably be above the 'maximum' mark (hot coolant expands). If the coolant level is OK, and there's no leakage, it's safe to carry on driving, but keep an eye on the temperature gauge! If the level is low, it's time to top up. You can use plain water in an emergency. If almost all the coolant has been lost, don't fill the cooling system with cold water whilst the engine is hot, as this might cause engine damage.

Fuel problems

If you run out of fuel, or if you fill up with the wrong fuel, don't panic – you're not the first to suffer this problem and things may not be as bad as they seem.

What to do if you run out of fuel

Don't keep on trying to start the engine, hoping to pick up the last drops of fuel from the tank – you'll suck air, and possibly dirt from the empty tank, into the fuel system, which will make starting even harder when you've filled up.

If you have a can of fuel, switch off the ignition and empty it into the tank. Operate the starter for short – say ten second – bursts, and if the engine now starts, drive on and fill the tank at the next filling station. If the engine still won't start, dirt or air drawn into the fuel system could be causing problems, in which case you'll probably need professional help.

If you're out in the middle of nowhere, or on a motorway, all's not lost – if you're a member of one of the motoring organisations, they'll deliver an emergency can of fuel to you.

If the fuel gauge indicated plenty of fuel in the tank, and you still ran out, have the gauge checked. If there's a fuel leak you should be able to smell the petrol vapour – don't drive the car until you've had the problem fixed.

On diesel engine cars, if you've run out of fuel the engine may be difficult to start even when you've refilled the tank. This is due to air being drawn into the fuel lines. Most cars are fitted with a hand priming pump (refer to your car's handbook) in the fuel system to get the engine started. Normally, the pump takes the form of a large pushbutton on top of the fuel filter, or a rubber bulb in one of the fuel lines. Switch on the ignition, then pump the priming button or bulb until you feel resistance (this could take more than 30 presses), indicating that the air has been expelled. Try to start the engine with the accelerator fully depressed – it should eventually start. If it still won't start, air has probably been drawn into the fuel injection pump, in which case you'll need to seek professional help.

What to do if you fill up with the wrong fuel

Diesel instead of petrol

Don't try to start the engine – if you do, it won't run for long, and you'll need to have all the fuel system components thoroughly cleaned and checked!

You'll need to have the fuel tank drained, cleaned and refilled with petrol before you can drive the car – call for help.

Petrol instead of diesel

If you've just put a few litres of petrol in the tank, stop filling with petrol, move to the diesel pump, and carry on filling with diesel. You won't have any problems.

If you've filled the tank with petrol, don't try to start the engine – if you do, it won't run for long, and you'll need to have all the fuel system components thoroughly cleaned and checked, which could be expensive!

You'll need to have the fuel tank drained, cleaned and refilled with diesel before you can drive the car – call for help.

Smoky exhaust

White smoke from the exhaust for a few seconds when you start the car first thing in the morning is no problem – it's just condensation from the exhaust turning into steam. The smoke should stop once the engine starts to warm up. Many diesel engines smoke heavily (black smoke) if you accelerate very hard after driving normally for a long time – again, it's nothing to worry about.

White smoke

Most often caused by coolant getting into the engine's cylinders, probably from a leaking cylinder head gasket. Often you'll be topping-up the coolant more than usual, and the engine oil level might seem to rise (as coolant leaks into it). This could be serious – have the problem checked out as soon as possible.

Diesel engines make a certain amount of white smoke when starting up, especially in cold weather. If it seems to be excessive, have the glow plugs checked.

On turbocharged engines, white smoke could be due to a leaking oil seal in the turbocharger. Have the problem checked out immediately, as the turbocharger will fail very quickly if the oil is leaking out.

Bluish white smoke

Usually caused by an oil leak inside the engine, this is normally due to worn valve-stem oil seals inside the cylinder head (not a huge problem), or worn engine bearings or cylinder bores (more serious). You'll often find that you're topping-up the oil more than usual. Have the engine checked before the problem develops into something serious.

Blue smoke on diesels can be caused by a problem with the fuel injection system. Get expert advice before jumping to conclusions.

Black smoke

Normally caused by too much fuel in the air/fuel mixture (if this happens on a car fitted with a catalytic converter, it could damage the catalyst very quickly, so don't drive the car any further than you have to). Black smoke is often accompanied by an increase in fuel consumption, and a black sooty deposit around the inside of the exhaust tailpipe. Have the problem checked out as soon as you can – the first thing to look for is a dirty air cleaner element.

It may be possible to fix things by making adjustments to the fuel system. If the problem goes on for too long it could cause engine damage.

Explaining a problem to a garage

If you've got a problem with your car, how do you explain it to the service manager or mechanic at the local garage? Remember that most garages will charge you at an hourly rate, so any extra information that you can give is likely to save you money in the long run.

If you haven't been able to identify a problem, here are a few things which you're likely to be asked when you take your car to the garage.

- Does the problem occur all the time, or is it intermittent?
- Does the problem occur when the engine's cold, hot or both?
- Are there any other symptoms (noises, vibration, etc)?
- Has the car been regularly serviced?
- Have you had any work carried out on the car recently?

If the problem occurs all the time, the best thing is to take the mechanic out for a drive and demonstrate it.

Intermittent problems can be difficult to trace and cure. If the problem is present for a while before disappearing, take the car to the garage when it's present. Most mechanical problems will be relatively easy to trace, but electrical problems can be tricky. Sometimes the garage may have no option but to renew various components until the problem disappears – this could prove to be expensive.

Always ask for a written firm price (sometimes it may not be possible to give an accurate final price), otherwise you may be faced with a large unexpected bill.

APPENDIX B
Glossary

The following guide is intended to help you to understand some of the more common terms that you'll come across when discussing your car with your local garage, or when talking to the local pub-bore!

ABS
Anti-lock Braking System. Uses sensors at each wheel to sense when the wheels are about to lock, and releases the brakes to prevent locking.

Air bag
An inflatable bag that inflates in the event of a sudden impact, to protect the driver and/or passengers from injury. Driver's air bags are usually mounted in the steering wheel and passenger's airbags are usually mounted in the dashboard. Some cars also have side-impact air bags, which may be mounted in various different locations.

Air conditioning
A system that enables the temperature of the air inside the car to be lowered, and dehumidifies the air. This allows more comfort and rapid demisting.

Air filter
A renewable paper or foam filter that removes foreign particles from the air that's sucked into the engine.

Airflow sensor
A sensor used in an engine management system to measure the amount of air being sucked into the engine.

Alternator
An electrical generator driven by the engine. It provides electricity for the car's electrical system when the engine's running, and to charge the battery.

Antifreeze
A fluid that's added to water to produce engine coolant. The antifreeze stops the coolant freezing in cold weather, and prevents corrosion inside the engine.

Anti-roll bar
A metal bar used in front and/or rear suspension systems to reduce the tendency of the car's body to roll from side to side. Not all cars have them.

Anti-seize compound
A grease coating that reduces the chances of seizing on components subjected to high temperatures and pressures.

Axle
A spindle on which a wheel revolves.

Ball bearing
A bearing consisting of two hardened metal rings, with hardened steel balls between them.

Balljoint
A maintenance-free flexible joint used mainly in suspension and steering systems to allow for movement of the components. Consists of a metal ball and cup, with a rubber seal to retain the grease.

Battery
A 'reservoir' that stores electricity. Provides the power to start the engine, and power for the electrical systems when the engine's stopped, and is charged by the alternator when the engine's running.

Bearing
A metal or other hard-wearing surface against which another part moves, and which is designed to reduce friction and wear. A bearing is usually lubricated.

Big-end
The lower end of a connecting rod which is attached to the engine's crankshaft. It incorporates a bearing, and transmits the movement of the connecting rod to the crankshaft.

Bleed nipple (or valve)
A screw, usually hollow, which allows fluid or air to be bled out of a system when it's loosened.

Bore
A term used to describe the diameter of a cylinder in an engine.

Brake backplate
A metal plate bolted to the rear suspension, which carries the rear brake components.

Brake bleeding
A procedure for removing air from the brake hydraulic system.

Brake caliper
The part of a disc brake system that houses the brake pads and the hydraulic pistons. The caliper straddles the brake disc.

Brake disc
A rotating metal disc coupled to a roadwheel, which is clamped between two brake pads in a disc brake system. As the brake disc slows down due to friction, so does the roadwheel.

Brake drum
A rotating metal drum coupled to a roadwheel. The brake shoes rub on the inside of the drum. As the brake drum slows down due to friction, so does the roadwheel.

Brake fade
A temporary reduction in braking power due to overheating of the brake friction material.

Brake fluid
A hydraulic fluid resistant to high temperatures, used in hydraulic braking systems and some hydraulic clutch systems.

Brake pad
A metal plate, with a pad of hard-wearing friction material bonded to one side. When the brakes are applied the hydraulic pistons in the brake caliper push the pads against the brake disc.

Brake servo
A vacuum-operated device that increases the force applied to the brake master cylinder by the brake pedal. Vacuum is supplied from the inlet manifold on a petrol engine, or from a vacuum pump on a diesel engine.

Brake shoe
A curved metal former with friction material bonded to the outside surface. When the brakes are applied the hydraulic pistons in the wheel cylinder push the brake shoes against the brake drum.

Breather
An opening or valve that allows air or fumes out of a system, or fresh air into a system.

Bucket tappet
A bucket-shaped cam follower usually fitted to the top of a valve.

Bump stop
A hard piece of rubber or plastic used in many suspension systems to prevent the moving parts from touching the body during suspension movements.

Caliper
See Brake caliper.

Cam belt
See Timing belt.

Camber angle
The angle at which the wheels are set from the vertical when viewed from the front of the car. Negative camber is when the wheels tilt inwards at the top.

Cam follower (tappet)
A component used to transfer the rotary movement of the camshaft lobes to the up-and-down movement required to operate the valves.

Camshaft
A rotating shaft driven from the crankshaft, with lobes or cams used to operate the valves, via the valve gear.

Camshaft lobes
Eccentric sections on the camshaft used to operate the valves via the valve gear.

Camshaft sensor
A sensor used in an engine management system to provide information on the position of the camshaft.

Carburettor
A device that's used to mix air and petrol in the correct proportions required for burning by the engine. Superseded on modern cars by fuel injection systems.

Castor angle
The angle between a front wheel's steering pivot axis and a vertical line through the centre of the wheel.

Catalytic converter
A device fitted in the exhaust system that reduces the amount of harmful gases released into the atmosphere.

Centrifugal advance
System for controlling the ignition timing using weights rotating on a shaft in a distributor which alters the ignition timing according to engine speed.

Choke
Either the device that reduces the amount of air entering a carburettor during cold starting (in order to provide extra petrol), or a term to describe the passage where the throttle valve is located in a carburettor.

Circlip
A ring-shaped sprung steel clip that locates in a groove to prevent lateral movement of cylindrical parts and shafts.

Closed loop
A term for an emissions control system using a catalytic converter where the engine management system controls the air/fuel mixture to allow the catalytic converter to operate at maximum efficiency.

Clutch
A friction device that allows two separate rotating components to be coupled together smoothly, without the need for either rotating component to stop moving.

Coil
See Ignition coil.

Coil spring
A spiral coil of sprung steel used in many suspension systems.

Combustion chamber
Shaped area into which the air/fuel mixture is compressed by the piston, and where the mixture is ignited. The combustion chamber may be formed in the cylinder head, or sometimes in the top of the piston.

Compression ratio (CR)
A term to describe the amount by which the air/fuel mixture is compressed as a piston moves from the bottom to the top of its travel. 10.0:1 CR means that the volume of mixture at the top of the piston travel is one tenth of the volume at the bottom of the piston travel.

Condenser
A component in an air conditioning system that condenses gaseous refrigerant into a liquid.

Connecting rod (con rod)
A metal rod in the engine connecting a piston to the crankshaft. The connecting rod transfers the up-and-down motion of the piston to the crankshaft.

Constant velocity (CV) joint
A joint used in driveshafts where the speed of the input shaft is exactly the same as the speed of the output shaft no matter what the angle of the joint.

Coolant
A liquid consisting of a mixture of water and antifreeze, used in a car's engine cooling system.

Coolant (water) pump
A pump driven by the engine that pumps the coolant around the cooling system.

Coolant sensor
A sensor used in an engine management system, or possibly in several other systems to provide information on the temperature of the engine coolant.

Cooling fan
Electric or engine-driven fan mounted at the front of the engine compartment and designed to cool the radiator.

CR
See Compression ratio.

Crankcase
The area of the cylinder block below the pistons, which houses the crankshaft.

Crankshaft
A cranked metal shaft that translates the up-and-down motion of the pistons and connecting rods into rotary motion.

Crankshaft sensor
A sensor used in an engine management system to provide information on the position and/or speed of the crankshaft.

Cubic capacity
The total volume inside an engine that's swept by the movement of all the pistons.

CV joint
See Constant velocity joint.

CVT
Continuously Variable Transmission. An automatic transmission with no fixed gear ratios. The gear ratios are constantly varied using a system of conical pulleys and a drivebelt.

Cylinder
A metal tube in the engine, in which a piston slides. The cylinders may be bored directly into the cylinder block, or cylinder liners may be fitted.

Cylinder block
The main engine casting, which houses the cylinders, crankshaft, pistons and connecting rods.

Cylinder head
The casting at the top of the engine that houses the valves and associated components. The cylinder head is bolted to the cylinder block.

Cylinder head gasket
A gasket fitted to provide a leak-proof seal between an engine's cylinder block and cylinder head.

Cylinder liner
A metal tube that fits inside the cylinder block to form the cylinder.

Damper
See Shock absorber.

Depreciation
The reduction in value of a car as time passes.

Derv
Abbreviation for Diesel-Engines Road Vehicle. A term often used for diesel fuel.

Diagnostic light (engine warning light)
A warning light on the instrument panel that illuminates when a fault code has been stored in the engine electronic control unit memory.

Diaphragm
A flexible membrane used in some components such as brake servos. The diaphragm spring used on clutches is similar, but is made from sprung steel.

Diesel engine
engine that relies on the heat produced when air is compressed to ignite the fuel, and so doesn't need an ignition system. Diesel engines have a much higher compression ratio than petrol engines.

Differential
A system of gears which provides drive to two wheels, but allows the wheels to turn at different speeds, for example during cornering.

Dipstick
A metal or plastic rod with graduated marks used to check the level of a fluid.

Direct injection
A type of fuel injection system where the fuel is injected by a fuel injector directly into the combustion chamber.

DIS

Direct Ignition System or Distributorless Ignition System. An ignition system that uses an electronic control module instead of a distributor.

Distributor

A device used to distribute the ignition HT circuit current to the individual spark plugs. The distributor may also control the ignition timing.

Distributor cap

A plastic cap that fits on top of the distributor, inside which the rotor arm rotates to distribute the HT circuit current to the correct spark plug. The cap contains electrodes (one for each cylinder).

DOHC

Double OverHead Camshafts. An engine with two camshafts, where one operates the inlet valves and the other operates the exhaust valves.

Drivebelt

A belt, usually made from rubber, used to transmit drive between two pulleys or sprockets. Often used to drive the camshafts and engine ancillaries.

Driveshaft

Term used to describe a shaft that transmits drive from a differential to one wheel.

Drivetrain

A collective term used to describe the engine/clutch/gearbox/transmission and other components used to transmit drive to the wheels.

Drum brake

See Brake drum.

Dual fuel

a term used for a car that is capable of running on two different fuels, normally LPG and petrol though some cars can run on CNG (Compressed Natural Gas) and petrol. Dual-fuel cars have two fuel tanks, one for each fuel.

Earth strap

A flexible electrical connection between the battery and the car's body, or between the engine/transmission and the body, to provide an electrical earth return to the battery.

EBD

Electronic Brakeforce Distribution. An electronically controlled braking system that ensures the braking force is distributed evenly between all four wheels to keep the car stable when braking. Usually combined with the ABS system.

ECU

Electronic Control Unit. A unit that receives electrical inputs from various sensors, processes the inputs, and produces electrical outputs to control one or more actuators.

EFI

Electronic Fuel Injection.

EGR

Exhaust Gas Recirculation. An emissions control system that recirculates a proportion of the exhaust gases back into the engine, where they are burnt with fresh air/fuel mixture.

Electrode

An electrical terminal, eg, in a spark plug or distributor cap.

Electrolyte

A solution of sulphuric acid and distilled water that conducts electrical current in a battery.

Emissions

Harmful substances (gases or particles) released into the atmosphere from a car's systems (usually the exhaust, fuel system or engine breather system).

Emissions control

A method of reducing the emissions released into the atmosphere. Various different systems are used.

Engine management system

A system that uses an electronic control unit to control the operation of the ignition system and fuel injection system, improving engine efficiency and reducing emissions.

Engine warning light

See Diagnostic light.

EVAP

An emissions control system on petrol-engined cars which stores vapour from the fuel tank and then releases it to be burnt, along with fresh mixture, by the engine.

Exhaust manifold

A device used for ducting the exhaust gases from the engine's cylinder head into the exhaust system.

Expansion tank

A container used in many cars' cooling systems to collect the overflow from the system as the coolant heats up and expands.

Fan belt

Another term for a drivebelt. The name arose because on older cars a drivebelt was used to drive the cooling fan. Electric cooling fans are used on most modern cars.

Fault code

An electronic code stored in the memory of an electronic control unit which gives details of a fault detected by the self-diagnostic system. A diagnostic light on the instrument panel will usually illuminate to indicate a fault.

Fault code reader

An electronic tool used to translate fault codes into a form that indicates where the fault lies.

Feeler gauges/blades

Thin strips of metal of a measured thickness used to check clearances between components, such as a spark plug gap.

Final drive

Another term used to describe a differential assembly.

Firing order

The order in which the pistons in the cylinders of an engine reach their firing points.

Firing point

The instant at which the mixture in the cylinder of an engine ignites in the combustion chamber.

Flat-engine

A form of engine in which the cylinders are positioned horizontally opposite each other, usually with an equal number on each side of the crankshaft.

Flywheel

A heavy metal disc attached to one end of the crankshaft in an engine, used to smooth out the power pulses from the pistons.

Four-stroke

A term used to describe the four operating strokes of a piston in a car engine.

Free play

The 'slack' in a linkage or an assembly of parts – for example, the distance the brake pedal moves before the master cylinder is actuated.

Friction disc

A metal disc with friction material attached to both sides used in a clutch assembly to progressively couple two rotating components together.

FSH

Full Service History. A written record which shows that a car has been serviced from new in accordance with the manufacturer's recommendations.

Fuel filter

A renewable filter that removes foreign particles from the fuel.

Fuel injection

A method of injecting a measured amount of fuel into an engine.

Fuel injection pump

A device that controls the quantity of fuel delivered to the fuel injectors in a diesel engine, and also controls the instant at which the injectors inject fuel.

Fuel injector

A device used to inject fuel into an engine. Some engines use a single fuel injector, whilst some use one fuel injector for each cylinder.

Fuel pressure regulator

A device that controls the pressure of the fuel delivered to the fuel injectors in a petrol fuel injection engine.

Fuel pump

A device that pumps fuel from the fuel tank to the fuel system.

Gasket

A compressible material used between two surfaces to give a leak-proof joint.

Gearbox

A group of gears and shafts in a housing used to keep a car's engine within its safe operating speed range as the speed of the car changes.

Glow plug

An electrical heating device fitted to a diesel engine to help it start from cold, and to reduce the smoke produced immediately after start-up. Each cylinder usually has its own glow plug.

Head gasket

See Cylinder head gasket.

Heater matrix
A small radiator mounted in the engine's coolant circuit that provides hot air for the car's heating system. Hot coolant flows through the matrix, which heats the surrounding air.

HT (high tension) circuit
The electrical circuit containing the high voltage used to fire the spark plugs in an ignition system.

HT (high tension) leads
Electrical leads which carry the HT circuit voltage to the spark plugs.

Hydraulic
A term used to describe the operation of a component or system by means of fluid pressure.

Hydraulic lifter (or tappet)
A valve lifter where the valve clearance is taken up hydraulically using oil pressure. This eliminates the need for valve clearance adjustment.

Idle speed
The running speed of an engine when the throttle is closed – ie, when the car is at rest and the driver isn't pressing the accelerator pedal.

Ignition coil
An electrical coil that generates the HT circuit voltage in a petrol engine ignition system to fire the spark plugs.

Ignition system
The electrical system that controls the spark used to ignite the air/fuel mixture in a petrol engine.

Ignition timing
A measure of the instant in the cylinder firing cycle at which ignition spark (provided by the spark plug) occurs in a petrol engine. The firing point is usually a few degrees of crankshaft rotation before the piston reaches the top of its stroke.

Independent suspension
A suspension system where movement of one wheel has no effect on the movement of the other, eg, independent front suspension or independent rear suspension.

Indirect injection
A type of fuel injection system where the fuel is injected by a fuel injector into a swirl chamber (diesel engine) or the inlet manifold (petrol engine) before entering the combustion chamber.

Inertia reel
Automatic type of seat belt mechanism that allows the wearer to move freely in normal use, but locks when the car decelerates suddenly or the wearer moves suddenly.

Injection timing
The instant in an engine's cylinder firing cycle at which fuel injection occurs.

Inlet manifold
A ducting, usually made of metal or plastic, which directs the air or air/fuel mixture into the engine's cylinder head.

In-line engine
An engine in which the cylinders are positioned in a row, instead of in a vee or flat configuration.

Input shaft
The shaft that transmits drive from the clutch to the gearbox in a manual gearbox, or from the torque converter to the transmission in an automatic transmission.

Jump leads
Heavy electrical cables fitted with clamps to enable a car's battery to be connected to another battery for emergency starting.

Kickdown
A device used on an automatic transmission that allows a lower gear to be selected for improved acceleration by fully depressing the accelerator pedal.

Knocking (Pinking)
A metallic noise from the engine often caused by the ignition timing being incorrect or a build up of carbon inside the engine. The noise is due to pressure waves that cause the cylinder walls to vibrate.

Knock sensor
A sensor that senses the onset of knocking and sends an electrical signal to the engine management system, to enable the ignition timing to be adjusted to prevent it.

Lambda sensor
See Oxygen sensor.

Laminated windscreen
A windscreen that has a thin plastic layer sandwiched between two layers of toughened glass. It will not shatter or craze when hit.

Lean
A term used to describe an air/fuel mixture containing less than the optimum amount of fuel.

LHM
A special type of mineral-based hydraulic fluid used in Citroën hydraulic systems.

Locknut
A nut used to lock another threaded component in place to prevent it from working loose.

Lockwasher
A washer designed to prevent a nut or bolt from working loose.

LPG
Liquefied Petroleum Gas. A mixture of liquefied petroleum gases, such as propane and butane, which are obtained from crude oil. Used in some engines as an alternative to petrol and diesel fuel.

MacPherson strut
An independent suspension component, which combines a coil spring and a shock absorber so that the swivelling, springing and shock absorbing for a wheel is carried out by a single assembly.

MAP sensor
Manifold Absolute Pressure sensor. A sensor that measures the pressure in the inlet manifold of a petrol engine and sends an electrical signal to the engine management system.

Mass airflow sensor
A sensor used in an engine management system to measure the mass of air being sucked into the engine.

Master cylinder
A cylinder containing a piston and hydraulic fluid, directly coupled to a foot pedal (or brake servo). Used for transmitting fluid pressure to the brake or clutch operating mechanisms.

Mixture
The air/fuel mixture burnt by an engine to produce power. In a petrol engine, the optimum ratio of air to fuel for complete combustion is 14.7:1.

Multi-point fuel injection
A fuel injection system that has one fuel injector for each cylinder of the engine.

Multi-valve
An engine with more than two valves per cylinder. Usually four valves per cylinder (two inlet and two exhaust valves), or sometimes three valves per cylinder (two inlet valves and one exhaust valve).

NOx
Oxides of Nitrogen. Toxic emissions found in the exhaust gases of petrol and diesel engines.

OBD
On-Board Diagnostics. A system that monitors the operation of the engine management system and records a fault code if any fault occurs within the system that may affect the exhaust emissions.

Octane rating
A scale rating for grading petrol. The higher the octane number, the more energy a given amount of petrol will produce when it's burnt by the engine.

OHC
OverHead Camshaft. An engine layout where the camshaft is mounted above the valves. Because the camshaft operates the valves directly (via the valve gear), an OHC engine is more efficient than an OHV engine.

OHV
OverHead Valve. An engine layout where the valves are located in the cylinder head, but the valve gear is operated by pushrods from a camshaft located lower in the cylinder block. Rare for modern engines.

Oil cooler
A small radiator fitted in the engine oil circuit, positioned in a cooling airflow or surrounded by coolant, to cool the oil. Often used on diesel engines and high-performance petrol engines.

Oil filter
A renewable filter that removes foreign particles from the engine oil.

Open-loop

A term for an emissions control system using a catalytic converter where the engine management system has no control over the air/fuel mixture.

O-ring

A type of sealing ring made of rubber. An O-ring is usually clamped between two surfaces (often into a groove) to provide a seal.

Overhead camshaft

See OHC.

Overhead valve

See OHV.

Oxygen sensor (lambda sensor)

Provides information on the amount of oxygen present in the exhaust gases. Used in a closed-loop catalytic converter system to enable the engine management system to control the air/fuel mixture.

PAS

Power-Assisted Steering. See Power steering.

Pinion

A term for a gear with a small number of teeth, which meshes with a gear having a larger number of teeth.

Pinking

See Knocking.

Piston

Cylindrical component which slides in a close-fitting cylinder. The pistons in an engine compress the air/fuel mixture, transmit power to the crankshaft via the connecting rods, and push the burnt gases out through the exhaust valves.

Piston ring

A hardened metal ring which spring-fits in a groove running around a piston. The piston ring ensures a gas-tight seal between the piston and the cylinder wall.

Plug

See Spark plug.

Power steering

A system that uses hydraulic pressure to provide assistance when the driver turns the steering wheel.

Pre-ignition

See Knocking.

Pressure cap

Acts as a cooling system safety valve by venting steam or hot coolant if the pressure rises above a certain level. Also acts as a vacuum relief valve to stop a vacuum forming in the system as it cools.

Propeller shaft

The shaft which transmits drive from the manual gearbox or automatic transmission to the differential on a front-engined, rear-wheel-drive car or to the rear and/or front differential on a four-wheel-drive car.

Pulse air

An emissions control system that introduces fresh air into the exhaust manifold through tubes, to raise the temperature of the exhaust gases. This in turn causes the catalytic converter to warm up more quickly.

Pushrods

Used on OHV engines (where the camshaft is mounted remotely from the valve gear) to operate the valve gear. The camshaft lobes act on the pushrods, which transfer the rotary movement of the camshaft lobes to the up-and-down movement required to operate the valves via the valve gear.

Rack-and-pinion

A form of steering mechanism where the steering wheel moves a pinion gear, which in turn moves a toothed rack connected to the roadwheels.

Radial tyre

A tyre where the fabric material plies (under the tread) are arranged at right-angles to the circumference of the tyre.

Radiator

A cooling device, located in a cooling airflow, through which a hot liquid is passed. A radiator is made up of fine tubes and fins to allow rapid cooling of the liquid inside.

Refrigerant

The substance used to absorb heat in an air conditioning system. The refrigerant is changed from a gas to a liquid and vice versa during the air conditioning process.

Release arm or lever

The device that transmits the movement of the clutch pedal to the clutch release bearing.

Release bearing

A bearing used to operate a clutch. It allows for the fact that the release arm or lever moves laterally, and the clutch components are rotating.

Rev counter

See Tachometer.

Rich

A term used to describe an air/fuel mixture containing more than the optimum amount of fuel.

Rocker arm

A lever used in an engine's valve-operating mechanism which rocks on a central pivot, with one end moved up and down by the camshaft and the other end operating a valve.

Rotary (Wankel) engine

An engine that has a triangular shaped rotor instead of the pistons used in a conventional engine. The rotor rotates in a housing shaped like a broad figure-of-eight. Some Mazda cars have this type of engine.

Rotor arm

A rotating arm in a distributor, which distributes the HT circuit voltage to the correct spark plug. An electrode on the rotor arm distributes the voltage to electrodes in the distributor cap, which are connected to the HT leads.

Running-on

A tendency for the engine to keep on running after the ignition has been switched off. Often caused by incorrect ignition timing, the wrong grade of fuel, or a poorly maintained engine.

Self-diagnostic system

A system that monitors the operation of an electronically-controlled system, and stores a fault code in the system electronic control unit memory if a fault is detected.

Semi-trailing arm

A common form of independent rear suspension.

Servo

A device for increasing the normal effort applied to a control. A brake servo increases the effort applied by the driver to the brake pedal.

Shim

A thin spacer, often used to adjust the clearance between two parts; for example, shims located under bucket tappets control the valve clearances.

Shock absorber

A device used to damp out the up-and-down movement of a wheel when the car hits a bump in the road.

Single-point fuel injection

A fuel injection system that has a single fuel injector.

16-valve

A term used to describe a four-cylinder engine with four valves per cylinder, usually two exhaust and two inlet valves. Gives improved efficiency due to improved air/fuel mixture and exhaust gas flow in the combustion chambers.

Slave cylinder

A cylinder containing a piston and hydraulic fluid, which receives hydraulic fluid pressure from a master cylinder, via a pipe, and uses movement of the piston to operate a mechanism.

Sliding caliper

A brake caliper that slides sideways in order to clamp the brake pads against the brake disc. A sliding caliper needs only one piston to operate both brake pads.

SOHC

Single OverHead Camshaft. An OHC engine with a single camshaft.

Solid rear axle

A rear suspension system where movement of one roadwheel directly affects the movement of the other.

Spark plug

A device that provides the spark in a petrol engine's combustion chamber in order to ignite the air/fuel mixture. The HT circuit voltage jumps between two electrodes on the spark plug, creating a spark.

Spark plug gap

The air gap between the electrodes on a spark plug.

Starter motor

An electric motor used to start the engine. A pinion gear on the starter motor engages with a large gear on the engine's flywheel, which turns the crankshaft.

Steering gear
A general term used to describe the steering components. Usually refers to a steering rack-and-pinion assembly.

Steering rack
See Rack-and-pinion.

Stroke
The total distance travelled by a single piston in a cylinder when it moves from the bottom to the top of its movement.

Strut
See MacPherson strut.

Stub axle
A short axle that carries one roadwheel.

Subframe
A small frame mounted underneath a car's body that carries the suspension and/or drivetrain assemblies.

Sump
The main reservoir for the engine oil. Bolted to the bottom of the engine.

Supercharger
A device that uses an engine-driven turbine (usually driven from the crankshaft) to drive a compressor which forces air into the engine. This increases the air/fuel mixture flow into the engine and increases the engine's power.

Suppressor
A device used to reduce or eliminate electrical interference caused by the ignition system or other electrical components.

Suspension
A general term used to describe the system that insulates a car's body from the roadwheels, and keeps all four roadwheels in contact with the road surface.

Swirl chamber
A device used in some types of diesel engine to swirl the fuel around to mix it with air before the mixture passes to the combustion chamber.

Synchromesh
A device used in a manual gearbox to synchronise the speeds of two gears to produce smooth, quiet engagement of the gears.

Tachometer (rev counter)
Indicates engine speed in revolutions per minute.

Tappet
See Cam follower.

Tappet adjustment
See Valve clearance.

TDC
See Top dead centre.

Thermostat
A device which aids engine warm-up by preventing the coolant from flowing through the radiator until a pre-determined temperature is reached. The thermostat then regulates the temperature of the coolant.

Throttle position sensor
A sensor used in an engine management system to provide information on the position of the throttle valve.

Throttle valve
A flap valve on a petrol engine, controlled by the accelerator pedal, located between the air cleaner and the inlet manifold. It controls the amount of air entering the engine.

Tie-rod
See Track-rod.

Timing belt (cam belt)
Toothed drivebelt used to transmit drive from the crankshaft to the camshaft(s).

Timing chain
Metal flexible link chain that engages with sprockets, used to transmit drive from the crankshaft to the camshaft(s).

Toe-in/toe-out
The angle at which the front wheels point inwards or outwards from the straight-ahead position when the steering is positioned straight-ahead. Toe-in is when the front edges of the wheels point inwards.

Top Dead Centre (TDC)
The exact point when a piston is at the top of its stroke.

Torque
The turning force generated by a rotating component.

Torque converter
A coupling used in an automatic transmission between the engine's flywheel and the transmission. The driving torque is transmitted through oil inside the torque converter.

Torque wrench
A tool used to tighten fasteners to an exactly measured torque (tightness).

Torsion bar
A metal bar which twists about its own axis. Used in some suspension systems.

Torx
A type of fastener, usually a screw or bolt, which needs a specially-shaped (Torx) socket or key to remove and refit it. Torx fasteners come in various standard sizes.

Track-rod (tie-rod)
A metal rod that connects the steering gear to a hub carrier. The track-rods move the front wheels when the steering wheel is turned.

Trailing arm
A form of independent suspension where the roadwheel is attached to a pivoting arm, with the wheel mounted to the rear of the pivot.

Transaxle
A combined gearbox/differential assembly from which two driveshafts transmit the drive to the wheels.

Transmission
A general term used to describe some or all of the drivetrain components excluding the engine. Commonly used to describe automatic gearboxes.

Turbocharger
A device that uses a turbine driven by the engine exhaust gases to drive a compressor which forces air into the engine. This increases the air/fuel mixture flow into the engine and increases the engine's power.

Twin-cam
Abbreviation for twin overhead camshafts – see DOHC.

Universal joint
A joint that can move in any direction whilst transmitting torque. Used in propeller shafts and some driveshafts. Not suitable for some uses because the input and output shaft speeds are not always the same for all angles of the joint.

Unleaded petrol
Petrol that had no lead added during manufacture, but still has the natural lead content of crude oil.

Vacuum pump
A pump driven by the engine that creates vacuum to operate the brake servo on a diesel engine.

Valve
A device that opens or closes to stop or allow gas or fluid flow.

Valve clearance
The clearance between the top of a valve and the camshaft, necessary to allow the valve to close fully and to allow for expansion of the valve gear components with temperature. Often adjusted by altering the clearance between the tappet and camshaft.

Valve gear
A general term for the components which are acted on by a camshaft to operate the valves.

Valve lifter
See Cam follower.

Vee-engine
An engine design in which the cylinders are arranged in two rows forming a 'V' when viewed from one end. For example, a V8 has two rows of four cylinders each.

Voltage regulator
A device that regulates the output of the alternator.

Wankel engine
See Rotary engine.

Water pump
See Coolant pump.

Wheel alignment
The process of checking the toe-in/toe-out, and sometimes the camber and castor angles of the wheels. On most cars only the toe-in/toe-out can be adjusted. Incorrect wheel alignment can cause tyre wear and poor handling.

Wheel balancing
The process of adding small weights to the rim of a wheel so that there are no out-of-balance forces when the wheel rotates.

Wheel cylinder
A slave cylinder used to operate the brake shoes in a drum brake.

APPENDIX C
Useful contacts

OFFICIAL BODIES

DVLA

Driver and Vehicle Licensing Agency
Longview Road
Swansea SA6 7JL
Website: www.dvla.gov.uk
Driver enquiries:
Tel: 0870 240 0009
Fax: 0870 850 1285
E-mail: drivers.dvla@gtnet.gov.uk
Vehicle enquiries:
Tel: 0870 240 0010
Fax: 0870 850 1285
E-mail: vehicles.dvla@gtnet.gov.uk

DSA

Driving Standards Agency
Stanley House
56 Talbot Street
Nottingham
NG1 5GU
Tel: 0115 901 2500
Website: www.dsa.gov.uk

MOTORING ORGANISATIONS

AA

Automobile Association
Member Administration
Contact Centre
Lambert House
Stockport Road
Cheadle SK8 2DY
Tel: 0800 085 2721
Fax: 0161 488 7300
Website: www.theaa.com

RAC

RAC Motoring Services
RAC House
1 Forest Road
Feltham TW13 7RR
Tel: 0800 731 7090
Website: www.rac.co.uk

Green Flag

Green Flag Motoring Assistance
Cote Lane
Pudsey
Leeds LS28 5GF
Tel: 0845 246 1557
Website: www.greenflag.com

Camping and Caravanning Club

Greenfields House
Westwood Way
Coventry CV4 8JH
Tel: 0845 130 7631
Website:
www.campingandcaravanningclub.co.uk

The Caravan Club

East Grinstead House
East Grinstead
West Sussex RH19 1UA
Tel: 01342 326944
Fax: 01342 410258
E-mail: enquiries@caravanclub.co.uk
Website: www.caravanclub.co.uk

IAM

The Institute of Advanced Motorists
IAM House
510 Chiswick High Road
London W4 5RG
Tel: 0208 996 9600
Fax: 0208 996 9601
Website: www.iam.org.uk

RoSPA

RoSPA House
Edgbaston Park
353 Bristol Road
Edgbaston
Birmingham B5 7ST
Tel: 0121 248 2000
Fax: 0121 248 2001
Website: www.rospa.org.uk

BUYING A CAR

Autoexpress

Website: www.autoexpress.co.uk

Autotrader

Tel: 08700 600 500
Website: www.autotrader.co.uk

British Car Auctions (BCA)

Tel: 0845 600 6644
Website: www.british-car-auctions.co.uk

Fish4Cars

Website: www.fish4cars.co.uk

HPI Ltd

Dolphin House
New Street
Salisbury
Wiltshire SP1 2PH
Tel: 01722 422 422
Fax: 01722 412164
Website: www.hpicheck.com

Manheim Vehicle Auctions

Tel: 0870 252 0400
Website: www.manheim.co.uk

Motability

Motability Operations
City Gate House
22 Southwark Bridge Road
London SE1 9HB
Tel: 0845 456 4566
Fax: 0207 928 1818
Website: www.motability.co.uk

Parkers Price Guide

Website: www.parkers.co.uk

What Car?

Haymarket Publishing
Teddington Studios
Broom Road
Teddington
Middlesex TW11 9BE
Tel: 0208 267 5685
Fax: 0208 267 5750
Website: www.whatcar.co.uk

Index